Paying Freedom's Price

The African American History Series

Series Editors:
Jacqueline M. Moore, Austin College
Nina Mjagkij, Ball State University

Traditionally, history books tend to fall into two categories: books academics write for each other, and books written for popular audiences. Historians often claim that many of the popular authors do not have the proper training to interpret and evaluate the historical evidence. Yet popular audiences complain that most historical monographs are inaccessible because they are too narrow in scope or lack an engaging style. This series, which will take both chronological and thematic approaches to topics and individuals crucial to an understanding of the African American experience, is an attempt to address that problem. The books in this series, written in lively prose by established scholars, are aimed primarily at nonspecialists. They focus on topics in African American history that have broad significance and place them in their historical context. While presenting sophisticated interpretations based on primary sources and the latest scholarship, the authors tell their stories in a succinct manner, avoiding jargon and obscure language. They include selected documents that allow readers to judge the evidence for themselves and to evaluate the authors' conclusions. Bridging the gap between popular and academic history, these books bring the African American story to life.

Volumes Published

Booker T. Washington, W.E.B. Du Bois, and the Struggle for Racial Uplift, Jacqueline M. Moore

Slavery in Colonial America, 1619–1776, Betty Wood

African Americans in the Jazz Age: A Decade of Struggle and Promise, Mark Robert Schneider

A. Philip Randolph: A Life in the Vanguard, Andrew E. Kersten

The African American Experience in Vietnam: Brothers in Arms, James Westheider

Bayard Rustin: American Dreamer, Jerald Podair

African Americans Confront Lynching: Strategies of Resistance, Christopher Waldrep

Lift Every Voice: The History of African-American Music, Burton W. Peretti

To Ask for an Equal Chance: African Americans in the Great Depression, Cheryl Lynn Greenberg

The African American Experience During World War II, Neil A. Wynn

Through the Storm, Through the Night: A History of African American Christianity, Paul Harvey

A Working People: A History of African American Workers since Emancipation, Steven A. Reich

Paying Freedom's Price: A History of African Americans in the Civil War, Paul D. Escott

Paying Freedom's Price

A History of African Americans in the Civil War

Paul D. Escott

ROWMAN & LITTLEFIELD
Lanham • Boulder • New York • London

Published by Rowman & Littlefield
A wholly owned subsidary of The Rowman & Littlefield Publishing Group, Inc.
4501 Forbes Boulevard, Suite 200, Lanham, Maryland 20706
www.rowman.com

Unit A, Whitacre Mews, 26-34 Stannary Street, London SE11 4AB

British Library Cataloguing in Publication Information Available

Library of Congress Cataloging-in-Publication Data

978-1-4422-5574-6 (cloth)
978-1-4422-5575-3 (electronic)

♾™ The paper used in this publication meets the minimum requirements of
American National Standard for Information Sciences—Permanence of Paper
for Printed Library Materials, ANSI/NISO Z39.48-1992.

Printed in the United States of America

In grateful memory of
Robert F. Durden
and
Raymond Gavins
historians, mentors, and friends

~

Contents

~

Chronology

1861

May 1861 Frank Baker, Shepard Mallory, and James Townsend escape from work on a Confederate fortification and turn themselves in to Union General Benjamin Butler, who declares them to be "contraband." Secretary of War Cameron endorses this policy, but for almost a year many Union officers return slaves to their rebel masters.

July 1861 The Northern Congress passes the Crittenden-Johnson resolutions, which state that the only purpose of the war is to restore the Union. Soon, however, the House of Representatives resolves that Union officers have no duty to capture and return runaway slaves.

July 1861 To the shocked surprise of Northerners, Confederates win the battle of Bull Run.

August 1861 Congress passes the First Confiscation Act, which declares forfeiture of slaves used in actual support of the rebellion. General John C. Frémont declares emancipation of slaves in Missouri. Lincoln overrules him.

Summer and fall 1861 Black men who offer to fight for the Union meet with rejection. The federal government as well as local officials tell them that the contest is a white man's war. Northern black leaders insist that the war must be a war against slavery.

November 1861 As Union forces occupy the Sea Islands, slaveholders flee. Some slaves go to work for Union forces; others farm for themselves. Educational efforts begin.

November 1861 Secretary of War Cameron proposes arming the slaves. President Lincoln modifies Cameron's final text. The House of Representatives passes a resolution favoring emancipation by the military of slaves of disloyal masters.

1862

February 1862 Northern blacks organize in their churches and other bodies to aid the contrabands. These efforts continue throughout the war. General Henry Halleck orders no admittance of runaway slaves into Union lines. Some commanders comply; others do not.

March 1862 Congress's new article of war prohibits soldiers from returning fugitives to their owners.

April 1862 Congress passes a law for compensated emancipation in the District of Columbia. Congress supports Lincoln's proposal to aid states that might adopt gradual, compensated emancipation with colonization.

April 1862 General David Hunter declares emancipation in his military district covering parts of South Carolina, Georgia, and Florida. Lincoln overrules him.

June 1862 Congress prohibits slavery in the territories.

July 1862 Lincoln appeals to border state congressmen to adopt gradual, compensated emancipation with colonization.

July 1862 Congress passes the stronger Second Confiscation Act and invites Lincoln to use freed slaves in the military.

Late summer 1862 Many black men are laboring for the U.S. army and navy; the number of black contrabands and refugees is increasing; black leaders continue to urge the use of African Americans in the military.

August 1862 Lincoln meets with several black leaders in the White House and unsuccessfully urges them to lead colonization efforts.

September 22, 1862 Lincoln issues his Preliminary Emancipation Proclamation.

Summer and fall 1862 A few black soldiers begin to enter the ranks in the Sea Islands, South Carolina, Louisiana, and Kansas.

1863

January 1, 1863 Lincoln issues the final Emancipation Proclamation.

March 1863 General Lorenzo Thomas goes to the Mississippi Valley to recruit black soldiers. The War Department establishes the American Freedmen's Inquiry Commission.

May 1863 The War Department establishes the Bureau of United States Colored Troops.

Summer 1863 Black soldiers fight bravely at Port Hudson, Milliken's Bend, and Fort Wagner. The number of black refugees usually exceeds the army's ability to care for them well. The government leases abandoned plantations in the Mississippi Valley to Northerners, and blacks work there as free laborers.

July 1863 Protests in New York City against the draft quickly become vicious antiblack riots. The border states remaining in the Union try to reinforce slavery, but soon army officers and officials start to ignore the claims of "loyal" slave owners.

Fall 1863 The War Department authorizes systematic enlistment of African Americans in Maryland, Missouri, and Delaware. In Kentucky slaves flee to nearby states to enlist.

1864

By this year African Americans' campaigns against segregation in streetcars or street railway lines had succeeded in most major Northern cities.

March 1864 Louisiana blacks meet with President Lincoln and press for their rights.

May 1864 The American Freedman's Inquiry Commission issues a final report that is supportive of black rights. Northern black leaders debate whether to support the reelection of Abraham Lincoln or to back a more progressive candidate.

July 1864 Lincoln issues his "To Whom It May Concern" letter stating conditions for peace. Northern whites' anger over the idea that emancipation now appeared to be a nonnegotiable war aim causes the administration verbally to retreat.

October 1864 Northern black leaders meet in convention in Syracuse, New York. They protest strongly against any retreat from racial progress by Lincoln or the Republican Party, and they demand equal rights. They found the National Equal Rights League. Maryland ends slavery in that state.

December 1864 Black leaders in Savannah, Georgia, meet with Secretary of War Edwin Stanton and General William T. Sherman.

1865

January 1865 General Sherman issues his Special Field Order Number 15. Soon forty thousand freed people occupy farms in the designated areas along the southeastern coast. Congress approves the Thirteenth Amendment abolishing slavery and sends it to the states for ratification. Missouri ends slavery there. African Americans in Tennessee petition the loyal government that is being formed there and seek justice.

February 1865 Reverent Henry Highland Garnet delivers a sermon in the halls of Congress to mark progress toward the Thirteenth Amendment. John Rock gains admission to the bar of the U.S. Supreme Court.

March 1865 Congress resolves that the families of black soldiers will be free; enlistments grow more. In Kentucky returning soldiers meet with extreme hostility.

April 1865 President Lincoln is assassinated. Freed blacks meet with white hostility throughout the defeated South.

June 19, 1865 West of the Mississippi River, many slaves receive official word, for the first time, that they are free. By this time Northern blacks have organized nine state branches under the National Equal Rights League.

Summer and fall, 1865 Freed Southerners organize in North Carolina, South Carolina, and elsewhere to petition for their rights from the all-white constitutional conventions required by President Andrew Johnson.

October 1865 Black farmers protest against President Johnson's decision to return the lands covered by Sherman's Special Field Order Number 15 to their formerly rebellious white owners. The National Equal Rights League meets in Cleveland, Ohio, demands the vote for Southern blacks, and calls for a constitutional amendment against laws that discriminate on the basis of race or color.

To end of 1865 U.S. army and Freedmen's Bureau try to suppress the general mistreatment of the freed people and liberate some illegally enslaved blacks.

December 1865 The Thirteenth Amendment is ratified.

~

Introduction

For African Americans, the Civil War marked an important turning point in a long and continuing struggle for freedom and equality. After generations of cruel enslavement, black people won their freedom. North and South, they rejoiced over this vital change. But they also suffered and paid a high price for pushing emancipation forward and defending the Union. Once free, they also faced the reality of a continuing struggle for social progress and equal rights.

When the Civil War began in 1861, African Americans had suffered enslavement in North America for more than two hundred years. In the wider Atlantic world, men and women kidnapped from Africa had performed forced labor as slaves for 350 years. The vast majority of these exploited human beings endured a life that was harsh, brutal, and short. Yet despite the vast amount of suffering, injustice, and resistance, few nations had questioned slavery.

It took many generations before societal change and new cultural values began to challenge the evil institution. But by the nineteenth century the emotional and intellectual climate had shifted. Western societies were coming to see slavery as a social, political, and moral problem. In 1787 the founders of the United States criticized human bondage but compromised with slavery, allowing it a place in the constitutional order. Thereafter conflicts related to slavery grew until they dominated the nation's politics. Northerners became more critical of slavery, while the South's white leaders defended the institution and blacks resisted it.

The long and destructive Civil War that began in 1861 created opportunities for freedom that black people, North and South, seized. African Americans took the initiative to transform America's internal conflict into a war for freedom. With their efforts, the war finally put a legal end to slavery in the republic and encouraged its retreat from the Western Hemisphere. It was a great victory. But the battle against racism and discrimination was not won, and it continues to the present day.

In pursuit of power and profit, European nations had created a ruthless system of exploitation that denied basic human rights. The Spanish and Portuguese began the cross-Atlantic traffic in African slaves as early as the sixteenth century. Later Britain and France became leading exploiters as their military and commercial power increased. The international "slave trade" transported almost ten million unwilling African slaves to New World colonies in the Caribbean and North and South America. Half of all imported slaves went to the Caribbean and Latin America; another large fraction became slaves in Brazil. In these areas they produced sugar to satisfy Europeans' sweet tooth, as well as coffee, cocoa, tobacco, rice, ore from mines, and other valuable commodities.

But the human costs were great. Those who survived a pestilential ocean crossing, crowded below decks amid their own excrement, faced a lifetime of coerced labor in new lands, amid strange people and strange cultures. The majority of Africans carried to the Western Hemisphere were young males. White slave owners valued them only for their muscle power, denied them a family life, and drove them so hard in the sugar islands that they often died within six or seven years. Without huge, continuing imports, slavery would have disappeared from the Caribbean.

The regions that became the United States were a smaller but integral part of the Atlantic slave trade and its web of commerce. Beginning in 1619, the first slave ships arrived along the Atlantic coast in the colony of Virginia. Before the American Revolution virtually every American colony, from Massachusetts to Georgia, held slaves. But the export crops slaves produced in colonial North America—tobacco, rice, and indigo principally, as well as firewood used for boiling syrup in the Caribbean—were never as profitable as the Caribbean's sugar. Fewer slaves arrived in British North America, and slaveholders learned that they needed to allow some kind of family groupings in order to profit from a natural increase among the enslaved population. Although slave marriages had no legal protection, North America's slave population grew substantially over time. Despite the fact that the areas that became the United States received only 6 percent of all slave imports in the New World, by 1825 the United States held the largest number of slaves in the entire Western Hemisphere.

Thus, a nation founded in liberty became the greatest slave power in the Western world. That contradiction produced two opposing tendencies in the United States. On the one hand, economic factors were increasing the power and reach of slavery. On the other hand, sentiment against slavery as a moral and political evil was growing.

The economic influence of slavery increased rapidly in the new nation. Many of the "Founding Fathers" had hoped that slavery would, somehow, die out in the United States. Instead it spread its tentacles deep into the economy and society, as the invention of the cotton gin put an end to those hopes. Britain's textile industry had an enormous and growing appetite for cotton fibers that were free of seeds. Eli Whitney's gin meant that short-staple cotton—which could be grown almost everywhere in the U.S. South—could feed the British demand.

Cotton exports soared, bringing wealth to many farmers and planters in the lower South. Eager to expand their production and gain more profit, slaveholders in the United States imported more slaves between 1780 and 1810 than in the previous 160 years. Hungry for new economic opportunities, white Southerners then expanded west into territories of rich soil bordering the Gulf of Mexico. In areas of the upper South, where slavery was not so profitable, slave owners were happy to sell human beings to areas of greater demand. The desire for wealth caused planters to buy more slaves and more land. Then, with their profits from exports, they rushed to repeat the process. Southern slaveholders came to produce three-quarters of the world's supply of cotton and 80 percent of all the cotton used by England. In the process they also built a repressive society organized in a multitude of ways around the defense of human bondage.

Economically, this "cotton kingdom" was a formidable power. By 1860 the market value of the South's enslaved human beings exceeded the total invested in banks by a factor of three. It was seven times greater than the sum of all currency in circulation in the country and forty-eight times greater than the spending of the federal government. From 1803 until well into the twentieth century, cotton was the leading U.S. export. The slave-based cotton economy supported eastern bankers and middlemen, New England textile mills and shoe manufacturers, and the U.S. shipping industry. Cotton had become extremely important to the U.S. and British economies, and those who depended on it were prone to defend and excuse slavery.

Yet by contrast the United States also was sharing in a broad movement of Western thought and feeling against enslavement. People became more sensitive to human suffering, and religious feelings and political ideals encouraged criticism of slavery. The United States itself had done much to spur the rising devotion to human rights. Its revolution against England began with the declaration in 1776 that "all men are created equal" and that they all have certain God-given "unalienable rights." The French Revolution, which began in 1789, gave added momentum to these ideals by stressing liberty, equality, and fraternity for all. In the 1790s slaves on the island of Haiti overthrew their masters and claimed freedom as their natural right. Britain was leading a campaign against the international slave trade, and by the 1830s and 1840s both Britain and France emancipated slaves in their colonies. Slavery was incompatible, as a matter of principle, with a belief in equality and human rights.

In the first decades after their revolution for independence, many Americans—even many individual slaveholders—recognized this moral incongruity. More than ten thousand slaves in the Chesapeake region gained their freedom, by their owners' decisions, in the 1780s and 1790s. These owners believed in the Revolution's ideals and concluded that they must free their human "property." Some condemned slavery in powerful language. Richard Randolph, a member of an important Virginia family, freed his slaves in his will, denouncing slavery as a tyrannical violation of human rights. Farther north, citizens, legislators, and judges felt the need to end a practice that had less economic importance and fewer defenders than in the South. By 1804 every Northern state had arranged—by laws of gradual emancipation or by court decisions—to dismantle the institution of slavery.

But the South's cotton boom stood in sharp contrast to the North's rejection of slavery—a contrast that foreshadowed future conflict. The potential for a sectional collision became evident in 1820, when Southern and Northern lawmakers clashed over the request by Missouri to enter the Union as a slave state. A Northern proposal to require gradual emancipation in Missouri set off a long and increasingly bitter debate. While Northerners asked how slavery could be reconciled with natural rights, Southerners denied the right of Congress to touch slavery at all. The Missouri Compromise did not settle the issue for all time but merely postponed an inherent conflict.

That conflict produced greater tension in the 1830s when a new abolitionist movement, influenced in part by religious fervor from the Second Great Awakening, arose in the North. Black and white abolitionists did not hesitate to brand slavery as a sin and call for its immediate abolition. Using the steam printing press and the new opportunities it created to spread their message, they distributed thousands of pamphlets, broadsides, and petitions. At first they were widely condemned and even attacked by mobs organized and led by "respectable" community leaders. Abolitionists remained a small minority of the total Northern population even on the eve of the Civil War. But steadily their efforts had an impact, as more Northerners became critical of slavery. Some citizens were moved by moral concerns. Others who felt less sympathy for the slave nevertheless came to see slavery as a threat to their self-interests.

Southern leaders moved in the opposite direction. Following the example of John C. Calhoun, they insisted that slavery was a "positive good." They argued that it was essential to their society and even the basis of freedom and equality among whites. Because they forced African Americans to do the most undesirable physical labor, all whites supposedly were equal as members of the superior race. The white South's defense of slavery also had a strong religious theme. Ministers took the lead in trying to justify slavery and supported it from their pulpits. Slavery was ordained by God, claimed leading members of the clergy. They preached that the Bible, God's holy word, sanctioned slavery, and to question it was to question the order and hierarchy that were a fundamental part of God's plan. In all respects they agreed with the politicians that slavery was a positive good.

Individual slaveholders tried to convince themselves that they treated their slaves kindly. They liked to talk about their biracial plantation "family." They congratulated themselves on doing their duty to supposedly helpless, inferior dependents. By asserting that the master-slave relationship was warm and affectionate, they protected themselves from criticism by Northerners and Europeans. For example, a wealthy North Carolina slaveholder claimed that the desire for profit would never cause him to be cruel or to risk the health of his slaves. The wives of slaveholders, even if they disliked some aspects of slavery, congratulated themselves on caring for idle and ignorant servants.

In return, African American slaves were supposed to be grateful, appreciative of the protection and guidance supposedly given them by their owners. There was a grain of truth in this claim. Many slaves and slave owners lived closely together day by day, a situation that fostered personal familiarity. In a region as large as the South, where millions of daily interactions took place, some blacks and whites developed mutual affection, loyalty, or concern for each other. These individuals treated their relationship as an exception to society's rules about slavery. Human beings are like that. But the overwhelming pattern was not what whites described and expected.

The South's slaves hated their bondage and the coercion on which it was based. They resented their owners, suspected their motives, and gave them little credit for the meager favors they received. Former slaves were eloquent and direct in their assessments of slavery. "It was hell," said one man.[1] Without freedom, they had to obey every white person's command or face unpleasant consequences. "It's bad to belong to folks that own you soul an' body," said Delia Garlic. "I could tell you 'bout it all day, but even den you couldn't guess the awfulness of it."[2] Another woman named Barbara Haywood tried to explain. "You ask if our white folks was good to us, an' I says to you that none of the white folks was good to none of the [slaves]."[3] In the same vein a man declared, "There was no such thing as being good to slaves. Many people were better than others, but a slave belonged to his master and there was no way to get out of it."[4]

The essence of slavery was more than hard work and the denial of liberty. It also was coercion, the physical compulsion or punishment imposed by owners or overseers. Slaves saw or experienced physical abuse daily or weekly—it was the plantation's primary force, and it came before the power of the state, embodied in laws, slave patrols, and militia. Slavery, as one woman recalled it, meant living under constant threat of the bullwhip. Being whipped at the master's discretion was an essential feature of slavery, and it was fiercely resented. Clay Bobbitt admitted that most of his whippings came when he refused to obey orders, but that was no justification. Bobbitt suffered abuse only because he was black and a slave.

Almost universally, the former slaves evaluated their masters according to how much cruelty they inflicted. A good owner was one who didn't beat them. But very few owners refused to use the whip. Occasional punishment of even one or two slaves, most slaveholders believed, helped to keep the others in line. A "nice" owner who did not whip earned the disapproval of his neighbors. As one slave recalled, all the whites who lived nearby criticized that slaveholder for ruining and spoiling his slaves. Bert Strong seems to have escaped whipping on his plantation, but he heard the screams of slaves on farms close by. What they suffered, he said, was terrible.

At the core of slaves' attitude toward owners, then, were resentment and suspicion. Slaves knew that they had created the wealth enjoyed by their masters—created it by their hard work and sweat. While their owners lived in comfort, slaves slept in rude cabins. While the master ate well, the slaves ate biscuits made from poor-quality, third-grade flour. While the white folks wore fashionable clothing, slaves made do with one or two outfits of rough osnaburg cloth. Many slaves believed that God would surely punish the slaveholders for their evil deeds. An ex-slave reported that many blacks in Virginia regarded an outbreak of yellow fever there in the 1850s as divine retribution on the whites. In Louisiana, when the two sons of a slave owner went off to war, the man broke down and cried. While he wept, his slaves felt joy, because they had suffered and cried from his cruelty many times.

The slaves suspected that motives of exploitation lay behind any type of good treatment that they received. Dosia Harris from Georgia knew why her mistress "was good to us"—"'cause she was raisin' us to work for her."[5] On another plantation where the owners provided ample food, one slave's grandmother asked, "Why shouldn't they?"[6]—after all, the slaves were a valuable investment. Presents of clothing, judged one slave, amounted to nothing because the master was going to buy the clothes anyway. Eli Coleman explained that his master "fed us reg'lar on good, substantial food, jus' like you'd tend to you horse, if you had a real good one."[7] Another man from Texas described his master as "purty good. He treated us jus' 'bout like you would a good mule."[8] Prudent owners took care of valuable slave "property" because it was their source of labor, but they denied the slaves' humanity and rights.

Such attitudes led to interference in slaves' family life and to sales and separations of loved ones. Mothers did not have much time to care for their children. On large plantations the older women, who no longer could do much work in the fields, watched little children while their mothers worked long hours and returned to their cabins, exhausted, at night. Planters often watched over pregnancies and births among the slaves with a greedy eye. One slave recalled that his owner cast an appraising look at the young children and bragged that some of them would be worth a thousand dollars or more when they grew up. With little or no reluctance, slave owners sold husbands away from their wives and parents away from their children. Slaves hated their bondage. Slaveholders presided over a suppressed but unhappy "family," and they worried over the slightest rumor of rebellion.

There were recurrent alarms about possible slave uprisings, and in 1831 Nat Turner led a rebellion in Southampton County, Virginia, that killed sixty whites. The South witnessed many other plots and conspiracies, most (but not all) on a smaller scale. But in North America the odds were against successful revolution. Whites were almost everywhere the majority, and a militarized, vigilant majority at that. There were few places for slaves to hide or escape to. The chances for successful revolt were not good, and slaves knew it. They took advantage, however, of every opportunity that came their way to limit the masters' power. Resistance was a constant part of life on the plantations.

Slaves resisted in a multitude of practical, daily ways. Some successfully ran away to the North, while others evaded the master's orders, learned to read, stole to supplement their diets, or found ways to support each other. Religion was an important source of strength for many. They worshipped in secret, where they could nourish their belief in a God of justice and reject the proslavery propaganda of white ministers. A deep sense of religious destiny gave them hope that God would end their servitude.

The mistreatment by slaveholders also taught many to rely upon and care for each other. Because they encountered hostility from almost every white, they instinctively knew to value their racial unity. The slaves were, in economic terms, an exploited class, but even more visibly they were a despised race—enslaved and mistreated because of the color of their skin. This fact gave them a useful, abiding suspicion of white people and a fierce desire to become free.

Still, white leaders stubbornly continued to defend the institution because slavery was the basis of the white South's wealth and was fundamental to the economy and social structure. Increasingly they insisted that the federal government must protect slavery, support its expansion, and do more to capture fugitives. No one could question slavery within the South. Few criticized mistreatment of slaves, and isolated, rural slaveholders were often free to abuse their slaves as they wished. On occasion the courts went so far as to say that "the power of the master must be absolute to render the submission of the slave perfect."[9]

Although all African Americans experienced discrimination, not all African Americans were slaves. On the eve of the Civil War, approximately 226,000 free blacks lived in the Northern states that had abolished slavery. They faced harsh prejudice—cradle-to-grave discrimination—in almost every Northern state. But their free status gave them certain precious advantages. African Americas in the free states could seek an education, worship in their own churches, organize for mutual aid and advancement, publish their own newspapers, practice a trade or profession, and open a business. Despite many obstacles, black people in the North made considerable progress. Leaders emerged who were well educated and financially successful. Ministers, abolitionists, and others started local and state organizations to work for abolition, equal treatment, and social progress. With protests and petitions to city councils and state legislatures, they fought for their rights. Some played an important role in the Underground Railroad that helped slaves escape to freedom. Others arranged for periodic national conventions, where the North's black elite discussed methods and took steps to benefit the entire race. African American leaders in the North had risen far compared to Southerners of their race, but they remained genuinely dedicated to helping their brothers and sisters in slavery.

A slightly larger population of free blacks lived in the upper and the lower South, and its members often had a respectable amount of property or considerable education. In areas of the upper South, such as Virginia, those who were free by 1860 usually were the descendants of men and women who had become free after the American Revolution. Many were farmers or laborers or watermen, but some had a skilled trade or business; all were careful to advance themselves, from one generation to another, in education and property holding.

In comparison to Virginia, the free black population of the lower South was much lighter-skinned, more urban, and better educated, as a consequence of its origin. At the time of the Revolution slavery had not spread into the Gulf region. But later on, after slaveholders established themselves there, wealthy planters sometimes fathered children by slave women. Some of these men felt a degree of parental responsibility for their offspring. When they acted on that feeling, they arranged for their children to become free, to gain a skill and practice a trade, and to receive an education. A portion of the free black children of white planters had attended colleges and universities in the United States or even in Europe. They would form a talented nucleus for leadership when slavery came to an end.

Among the lower South's slaves, there also were men and women of intelligence and insight who had managed to educate themselves. The percentage who were literate was well under 10 percent, but some had found sympathetic whites who would help. Others snatched at any piece of reading material to practice and learn. Despite slavery's cruelties—not just the denial of freedom and exhausting demands of work, but also physical abuse, sexual exploitation, and the separation of families—some slaves would be well prepared for leadership.

The Civil War affected African Americans in different parts of the United States in different ways. But it also brought them closer together and demonstrated the powerful desire for freedom, opportunity, equal rights, and equal treatment that they all shared. The war years proved to be a period of great, historic progress for African Americans. They also were a time of great struggle, sacrifice, tragedy, and disappointment. By the end of 1865, black Americans had gained a great prize: freedom. But they also had paid a high price and suffered terrible losses in reaching this goal. Along with enormous joy, they experienced great disappointment. And they still faced a long battle to end discrimination and to win equal rights, full citizenship, and dignified treatment.

Notes

1. Quoted in Paul D. Escott, *Slavery Remembered: A Record of Twentieth-Century Slave Narratives* (Chapel Hill: University of North Carolina Press, 1979), 36.
2. Ibid., 38.

3. Ibid., 27.
4. Ibid.
5. Ibid., 24.
6. Ibid.
7. Ibid., 25.
8. Ibid., 26.
9. *State v. Mann*, 13 North Carolina Reports 263 (1829).

CHAPTER ONE

~

Forcing the Issue

Wars bring surprising changes. The Civil War transformed the United States, destroying slavery and moving the nation one long stride closer to its founding ideals of freedom and human equality. Yet it began as a struggle to preserve the status quo. Southern leaders, wealthy rulers of the most extensive slaveholding society in the Western Hemisphere, left the Union to protect slavery. Northerners went to war to keep the Union intact, not to end human bondage. But Northerners found that victory was uncertain, and slaves yearned for freedom. As a result, the Civil War became something else—a tidal wave of change that advanced human rights by ending slavery in a nation addicted to racism.

African Americans, North and South, played a crucial role in this transformation. By taking great risks and striking out for freedom, they forced the issue. Slaves ran away, and free blacks agitated for freedom and equality. Meanwhile, military defeats and setbacks shocked the North, causing opinions about the purpose of the war to change. Northerners began to see that slavery's foes were right—to win the war, the North had to strike at slavery. These two factors redefined a war that had been about the status quo. It became a war for freedom, even though racial prejudice seemed unshakable. By seizing the initiative and taking advantage of the Union's military needs, African Americans forced emancipation onto the nation's agenda.

The 1850s had been a discouraging decade for African Americans. It had been an especially discouraging time for the minority of black and white

Northerners who were abolitionists. But the events of that decade inspired a new political party that—though not abolitionist—was at least opposed to slavery's growing power. Throughout the 1850s slavery won many battles, advancing and gaining strength both economically and politically. The ruthless exploitation of black Southerners fueled a major part of the American economy and was the source of increasing wealth for the South. The world wanted cotton cloth, and factories in England and New England devoured all the white fibers that black hands could grow. Politically, the dominant issue in American life was the future of the territories—the Great Plains, the Northwest, and the vast southwestern lands obtained in a war with Mexico. The South was winning each struggle over those territories.

Wherever they could, black leaders denounced these alarming trends. Frederick Douglass, the former slave who became an eloquent speaker, writer, and editor, warned Northerners to wake up. Slavery, he said, was the enemy of democratic institutions, and white Northerners should fight against efforts that would allow slavery to spread. Other black leaders continued their fight against slavery in the South and rampant discrimination throughout the North. But the progress of slavery interests convinced a few African Americans that it would be best to leave the United States—to immigrate to some other land in order to escape discrimination and gain a fair chance to demonstrate what black people could accomplish. For a brief period even Douglass spoke favorably about emigration from the United States.

The march of the Slave Power also alarmed many white Northerners, though their fear of slaveholders did not have to involve any respect for African Americans. President James K. Polk had already disappointed Northerners by reducing the nation's claims to land in the Oregon territory. Then in 1846, Congressman David Wilmot focused attention on the Southwest. Wilmot, a Pennsylvania Democrat, offered a proviso, or amendment, to a bill that would fund the army during the Mexican War. The purpose of the proviso was to prohibit slavery from any lands in the Southwest won from Mexico. As Wilmot explained in Congress, California and the Southwest should be reserved for free white settlers. He openly declared that he had no sympathy for enslaved African Americans and ridiculed the idea that people should feel troubled by their bondage. He was after more opportunities for his own race, for people of his own color. Many Northerners agreed that the territories should be for whites—fourteen Northern state legislatures endorsed his proviso. But due to Southern opposition, Congress never passed the proviso, and the Compromise of 1850 failed to include Wilmot's idea. It did not prohibit slavery from the Southwest.

The Compromise of 1850 seemed bad enough to Northerners, especially when they realized that its new fugitive slave law forced them to help in the capture of runaway slaves. Then, in 1854, the Kansas-Nebraska Act overturned the Missouri Compromise and opened the Great Plains to slavery. Thousands of white farmers interested in western lands felt threatened. The Republican Party, an entirely new organization, was born from their protests. We cannot allow slavery in the unorganized territories, said Republicans. Abraham Lincoln emphasized the importance of the territories, explaining that they should be reserved for white people, and later he warned of a conspiracy to impose slavery on the free states.

Republicans were critical of slavery and branded it as a danger to the nation. Lincoln called slavery a great injustice and raised a moral question: if the Negro was a man, did he not have some rights? But Lincoln's party rejected racial equality and staunchly defended the right of slavery to continue in the states where it already existed. Lincoln explained that his own feelings were opposed to political or social equality for African Americans. Other Republicans insisted that blacks and whites could not live together in freedom. Colonization—removal of African Americans to some other country—was essential, they said, if slavery ended. On various occasions Lincoln himself spoke favorably about colonization.

The rise of this new Republican Party frightened slaveholders. They argued that slavery must have a right to expand and enter any territory. The Supreme Court came to their support. In the Dred Scott decision in 1857, the court declared that black people were not citizens, that Congress could not prohibit slavery from any territory, and that the Missouri Compromise of 1820—which barred slavery from most of the Louisiana Purchase—had never been constitutional. Southern leaders then became even more adamant in their demands. They argued that the Constitution guaranteed slavery's status in the territories. One of Mississippi's senators warned Congress that the South would insist on expanding slavery.

Northerners, in turn, were shocked. As a Cincinnati newspaper put it, Slave Power seemed to be gaining complete control of the nation's government. "Where will it end?" asked the *Atlantic Monthly* magazine. "Is the success of this conspiracy to be final and eternal?"[1] Abraham Lincoln warned that slavery might be imposed even on the free states. He described a proslavery conspiracy designed to make slavery legal in the North as well as the South.

The first Republican presidential candidate, John C. Frémont, won many Northern states in 1856. In 1860 Lincoln won the presidency by dominating the Northern vote and gaining a majority in the electoral college. Though Lincoln received less than 40 percent of all ballots cast, he became president. South Carolina promptly seceded, citing the election of an antislavery president as the cause. Georgia followed, complaining of acts against slavery, and alleging they were efforts to incite the slaves to rebellion. Mississippi declared that slavery was such a part of the state's identity that it had no choice but to secede. With similar statements, four other Gulf states rapidly followed. Before Lincoln could take office, seven slaveholding states had left the Union.

In his inaugural address, Lincoln pledged to preserve the Union and said slavery was wrong. But he promised to protect slavery where it already existed. He even gave his support to a proposed constitutional amendment that would guarantee that the Federal government could never interfere with slavery in the Southern states. It was not enough. The newly organized slave-holding Confederacy fired on Fort Sumter, in South Carolina, in April 1861, and war began. Virginia, North Carolina, Tennessee, and Arkansas then joined the Confederacy, and the Union was locked in battle with eleven of the fifteen slaveholding states.

Just as defending slavery was the Confederacy's purpose, it was equally clear that the North went to war only to preserve the Union. Echoing Lincoln's promises in his inaugural address, the U.S. Congress promptly declared that the North fought only to preserve the Union, with proper respect for the rights of the states. The North had no purpose or plans to interfere with slavery in the rebellious states. The struggle, then, was over whose version of the status quo would prevail.

But African Americans—enslaved and free—thought differently. In both South and North, they pressed to change the agenda. Three slaves from Virginia were the first to show the way. In May 1861 they appeared at Fort Monroe, an isolated Federal post on Chesapeake Bay. They had escaped across the water in a stolen rowboat from Confederate-held territory, where they had been forced into building a position for large cannons. Escaping from the Confederates was risky enough, but in addition these slaves could not know how the Federals would receive them. Both President Lincoln and Congress had pledged not to interfere with slave property, and army officers were returning runaway slaves to their owners.

Union soldiers took these men—Frank Baker, Shepard Mallory, and James Townsend—to see the fort's commander, Major General Benjamin Butler. They told him all they knew about the enemy's preparations, and they offered to help the Union. Then a Confederate major, who arrived under a flag of truce, helped Butler decide what to do. The major demanded that Butler honor his constitutional obligation and return the slaves. But since Virginia had seceded and claimed it was no longer part of the Union, Butler saw no such obligation. He decided to keep the runaway slaves as

Nothing could stop the tide of slaves escaping into Union lines—like these who sought freedom near Culpeper Court House, Virginia. Library of Congress, Prints and Photographs Division.

"contraband of war"—an enemy asset he could seize. Their labor would help the Union, not the Confederacy.

Frank Baker, Shepard Mallory, and James Townsend had begun an exodus that white Confederates could not stop. Wherever Union forces entered Confederate territory, slaves started running away from their masters in hopes of gaining freedom. Once within Union lines, they proved that they were eager to help the North. Not all commanders would act as Benjamin Butler had done. Official policy required the return of slave "property." But that did not stop the widespread flight from slavery, and Butler's logic was unassailable. African Americans could help the Northern war effort.

Quite a few Northern newspapers hailed General Butler's decision to keep and use black contrabands. It simply made sense as a tool to win the war. Every slave added to the Union war effort was a laborer subtracted from the Confederacy. And it quickly became apparent that the number of laborers could be enormous. Every Union military camp was a magnet for runaway slaves. Hungry for freedom, they were ready to trade bondage for an uncertain new status as contrabands. "Their great, soul-hungering desire was freedom," recalled one ex-slave.[2] As another slave who escaped into Maryland explained, "All we wanted was a chance to escape."[3]

Elsewhere many free blacks were thinking about ways to help the Union cause. Black Ohioans offered to defend the national government. African Americans in Massachusetts asked the state's legislature to remove the word "white" from the laws that established state militias so that they could enlist and demonstrate their loyalty. An important black newspaper, New York City's *Weekly Anglo-African*, predicted that the fight would end in freedom for the enslaved, and Frederick Douglass predicted that "the 'inexorable logic of events' will force" the government to see that the contest "is a war for and against slavery."[4]

Harsh reality soon became an important factor in changing white Northern attitudes toward slavery. Defeat in the war's first major land battle—the Battle of Bull Run in July 1861—came as a shock to overconfident Northerners. Government officials and picnickers who had ridden out from Washington to watch a great Union victory suddenly had to flee in panic from Confederate forces. Such an unpleasant surprise increased resentment of slaveholders as the cause of the war and raised the stakes. Realizing that victory would not come easily, the Congress took its first, limited step against slavery. Departing from its earlier proslavery resolution, Congress passed the First Confiscation Act, which said that Southern slave owners would forfeit their claim to any slave used in direct support of the rebellion.

But progress against slavery was slow. Soon opposition arose to using the labor of contrabands or taking further actions against slavery. White racism was a potent force. Philadelphia's chief of police told African Americans who wanted to join the army that the war was a white man's war. In New York City some black men began to practice military drill, only to have the chief of police order them to stop, saying he could not protect them from mob violence. The same thing happened in Cincinnati, where black men organized a company to help defend the city. The police ordered them to keep out of the fight because they had no place in a white man's war. The commander of Ohio's militia refused to consider any black volunteers and pointed out that the law prohibited their service.

Few Republican politicians wanted to challenge these racist attitudes. Abraham Lincoln had, in addition, another concern. He realized that winning the war would be difficult, and he needed to hold on to the Union's four slaveholding border states—Delaware, Maryland, Kentucky, and Missouri. Maryland's factories were vital to the railroad industry. Kentucky and Missouri had large populations and contained resources of men and material that could be extremely valuable to the Confederacy. These states were still in the Union, but many of their white citizens were sympathetic to the South. Lincoln resisted a controversial, unpopular measure such as accepting black recruits, although it would be a blow to slavery and a step toward racial equality. Thus, his administration's policy was to wage a white man's war. The secretary of war told black volunteers that the government had no intention to use black soldiers.

Such rejection naturally angered patriotic African Americans who had been ready to risk their lives for the Union. Henry Cropper had been chosen captain of a unit of black volunteers, but rejection of his company convinced him that they must protest such racism. He resolved only to serve if it were on equal terms with all men. Others felt they should not offer their service only to be insulted and abused. The *Christian Recorder*, published by the African Methodist Episcopal Church, concluded that to try to enlist would be to invite insults and lose self-respect. A correspondent of the *Weekly Anglo-African* asked why black men should consider dying if the war would not bring them freedom and counseled neutrality unless the government offered to end slavery.

For many months President Lincoln's policies remained discouraging. He refused to take steps directly against slavery. In August 1861 John C. Frémont, who was the commanding general in Missouri, declared martial law and emancipation there for all slaves belonging to rebels. Initially many Republican newspapers praised Frémont's action and were pleased that Frémont was treating rebellion as a crime. But quickly Lincoln overruled Frémont to avoid offending Kentuckians or alarming any Southern Unionists. Loyal Republican newspapers had to backtrack to support their president. Northern blacks felt no such constraint, and they voiced their dismay and anger. Reverend J. P. Campbell, a high official in the African Methodist Episcopal Church, declared in disgust that Lincoln was no abolitionist and did not even deserve to be called an antislavery man. The editor of the *Weekly Anglo-African* condemned Lincoln's decision for returning to slavery's hell the thousands in Missouri whom General Frémont had rightfully freed.

Late in the fall of 1861 Lincoln put forward some proposals for federally compensated, gradual emancipation through voluntary state action. To state legislators in Delaware, where there were few slaves, he proposed a gradual process that could take only five years or go on until 1893. Lincoln favored the longer period, and his proposal included apprenticeship for young children that would continue until age eighteen or twenty-one. Delaware's lawmakers narrowly rejected the idea. Then, in his annual address to Congress in December 1861, Lincoln proposed that the thousands of slaves pouring into Union lines and the District of Columbia should be considered free.

But he also proposed that steps should begin to colonize them in some warm climate. He even went on to say that colonization could include all African Americans who had been free before the war.

Discouraging though the government's policy was, many of the best-known black leaders continued to urge support of the Union and argued to whites that the war must be a war against slavery. J. W. C. Pennington, a prominent black preacher and lecturer, circulated a petition branding slavery the cause of the nation's crisis. He called on Congress to take measures to abolish slavery immediately. Frederick Douglass argued that "*the simple way*" to save the Union "*is to strike down slavery itself*, the primal cause of the war."

Frederick Douglass, who escaped from slavery to become a leading abolitionist, argued forcefully for emancipation and the use of black soldiers. Library of Congress, Prints and Photographs Division.

He called the Negro "the key of the situation." Slave labor was a "mighty element of strength" to the rebels. Why, he asked, "does our Government allow its enemies this powerful advantage. . . . The national edifice is on fire. Every man who can carry a bucket of water, or remove a brick, is wanted."[5]

Like Douglass, most of the North's black leaders also turned against the idea of emigration or colonization. They believed that the war would likely damage or destroy slavery, and such an opportunity to bring freedom to the slaves was too precious to pass up. Their task was to agitate for freedom and for the right of black men to fight for the Union. In that way they would advance freedom *and* black rights. Increasingly they agreed with John Rock, a doctor, dentist, and lawyer who lived in Boston. "This being our country," Rock declared, "we have made up our minds to remain in it, and to try to make it worth living in." The energies required for emigration should instead be devoted to "working our way up in this country, and in civilizing the whites." Rock and the large majority of black leaders would insist that "this is our country."[6]

Meanwhile, in the South slaves were showing in additional ways that their actions could force a change in the agenda. They took actions to help the Union that went beyond the labor of contrabands. Allan Pinkerton, chief of the U.S. Secret Service, traveled secretly to Memphis in 1861 on a spy mission. There he found many slaves forced to aid the Confederacy by building earthworks and fortifications, driving teams of horses, and transporting and unloading weapons and ammunition. But Confederate slaves were very ready to help this Union spy. Pinkerton found that they were his best source of information. They were always ready to answer his questions, and they gave him every fact that he needed to have. This was merely one early example of the valuable information slaves could bring. That June a black man named William Tillman brought something more valuable. Tillman, who had been serving as steward on a schooner captured by the Confederacy, took control of the boat at night, killed some of the rebels on board, and sailed it into New York harbor with the Union's flag proudly flying.

Lincoln's first secretary of war, Simon Cameron, saw that slaves were helping the Union. He also was impressed by the logic of Frederick Douglass's arguments. Why let the South benefit from slave labor, when slaves could serve the Union? How might they best help the Union cause? To Cameron, the answer was plain. In his department's annual report of November 1861, Cameron recommended arming the slaves.

This idea was too much for Abraham Lincoln, still worried about the border states. As soon as Lincoln learned of this recommendation, he ordered that Cameron drastically tone it down. But the original version had already reached some newspapers. The idea of using African Americans as soldiers was gaining a little ground, and the House of Representatives passed a resolution favoring emancipation by military action of slaves whose owners were disloyal. The logic of events, plus slaves' desire for freedom, was beginning to bring change. Congress would move more quickly than the president, but the policies of both evolved.

The status of contrabands, however, first went through a period of confusion. How the military treated contrabands in 1861 and early 1862 varied, depending on where the U.S. army operated and what policies were in effect. When the army advanced into Kentucky and Maryland—states that had not seceded—the government's priority was to avoid giving offense to slaveholders. Accordingly, policy there required commanders to return runaway slaves to their masters, who were assumed to be loyal, putting slaves in a terrible position. Those who tried to gain their freedom took great risks in escaping from their owners to reach a Union position. Then, if they made it safely, they found that the Union did not give them freedom but returned them—to an angry slaveholder. In such circumstances, their situation was worse than it had been before.

Along the coast of South Carolina, however, on the Sea Islands, the facts were different. When Union ships and troops arrived in November 1861, the owners of these coastal plantations fled, leaving their slaves behind. These men and women suddenly could enjoy the taste of freedom and make decisions for themselves. The army offered wages to those who would harvest the cotton that was in the fields. Many did that work and then began to farm for themselves. Army officers next tried to recruit them to do various jobs for the army. But when the government failed to offer decent wages, as it often did, most chose to continue farming on their own. Before long Northern abolitionists and businessmen arrived in the Sea Islands to encourage experiments in free labor. The abolitionists' priority was to help and to educate the slaves, who were eager for schooling. The businessmen proved to be more interested in profits and were sometimes guilty of sharp dealing.

As the Union army gained a small foothold in other Southern states, such as North Carolina, Virginia, Arkansas, Tennessee, and Louisiana, different patterns developed. But the behavior of the slaves was always the same. Everywhere they left their plantations in large numbers and came, with determination and enthusiasm, into Union lines. These "contrabands" wanted to be free, and they were eager to help the Union army, which they recognized as a liberating force. Most men went to work doing all sorts of heavy labor for the military, while others, including the women, helped individual soldiers as cooks or laundresses. The desire for freedom was unstoppable, and it advanced the goal of destroying slavery.

Army officers reacted in various ways to this growing tide of fugitives, with some welcoming the labor that runaway slaves could offer. But other commanders worried about the increasing numbers who came into camp. Where were they to put these runaways? And what was the army to do with the women and children who often accompanied their men? How would they feed them, or give them shelter? The slaves escaped under urgent and dangerous circumstances. In many cases they arrived with no food or possessions and wearing only the tattered clothing on their backs. Caring for hundreds of needy people seemed a burden to some white officers. Other commanders worried that the numbers of contrabands in camp would interfere with military efficiency and movement.

The question was political for some generals. George B. McClellan was a Democrat who wanted to protect slavery. Predictably, his policies favored returning slave "property" whenever possible. In the fall of 1861 McClellan, who was then general-in-chief, encouraged several western generals to bar runaway slaves from their lines. Early in 1862 General Henry Halleck, then commanding in the west, ordered his subordinates to keep slaves out of their camps. Halleck wanted to reassure rebels that the army would return their "property" as it had done in the past. Like Halleck, many commanders felt that it was not up to the military to decide on the issue.

Others disagreed. The courage of the slaves impressed many soldiers. Despite widespread racism, there were many lower-ranking officers who felt sympathy for exploited people who defied danger and took many risks to reach the army, hoping for freedom. To turn them away seemed cruel and heartless. Accordingly, such officers allowed them to stay and found useful tasks for them. Other commanders felt they needed the fugitives' labor and were glad to accept at least some of the slaves' offers to help. For example, General Ulysses S. Grant gave orders that dependent women and children should be kept out of camp. But he welcomed strong men who could labor for his army. General Ambrose Burnside in Virginia ignored any policies against accepting contrabands. In Louisiana a commander from Vermont disputed his orders to exclude runaways, protesting that he had not gone to war to send men into slavery. In the border states officers wondered how they had the time or the means to distinguish a free African American from a runaway slave.

The question of how to treat the runaways became a public controversy, as newspapers and Congress debated what to do. Racism also became a force that skewed politics and threatened to affect the 1862 elections. On the one hand, the logic of using slaves to help the Union and hurt the rebellion was gaining ground. Elements in the Republican Party that were strongly against

slavery saw an opportunity and pressed for a change in policy. They succeeded in March 1862, when Congress passed a new article of war. This regu-
lation prohibited soldiers from returning fugitives to their Southern masters.
From that point forward, the army had to allow runaway slaves to stay within
the Union lines, where they could enjoy some new measure of freedom.

On the other hand, to welcome contrabands aroused racist fears and criti-
cisms. The Democratic Party and its newspapers repeatedly criticized contraband camps, where the army provided some form of food and shelter for runaway slaves. The cost of supporting these contrabands, Democrats claimed, was
astronomical. They charged that the government was burdening white citizens
with heavy taxes and massive debt, just to allow ignorant, inferior, escaped
slaves to live in idleness. Appealing to racism, Democratic newspapers claimed
that the government was favoring lazy blacks over virtuous whites.

In fact, the situation for the contrabands was often a difficult one. Dependent women and children, as well as the men, sought to be an asset to
the Northern war effort. They found many ways to help the Union army,
by cooking, mending, washing clothes, or performing various types of labor.
But conditions in the contraband camps frequently were bad—crowded, unhealthy, or with inadequate food and shelter. A Union officer admitted that
a camp hospital in Arkansas was notorious for filth, neglect, a high death
rate, and even for brutal whippings that occurred there. Still, thousands were
gaining freedom as runaways poured into Union lines.

Hostile reaction was even worse when some commanders decided to send
contrabands into the North. These officers wanted to solve the problems
that the growing number of runaways posed for the military. Its primary job
was to fight a war, rather than to arrange food, shelter, and useful work for
Southern slaves, and it sometimes lacked the means to do both. In September 1862 Ulysses S. Grant, then commanding the Department of the Tennessee, sent several hundred women and children to Cairo, Illinois. With the
assistance of various charities, arrangements were made there to hire these
people in various midwestern states. General John A. Dix, then commander
at Fortress Monroe, similarly asked several governors to help him relocate
slaves into the Northeast. Other runaways who were being housed in St.
Louis were sent north or west to work. Due to the war, there was a demand
for labor in various Northern states where businesses had lost employees to
the army. Well-to-do housewives also wanted servants to help them with
the cooking and cleaning. A Minnesota resident said that the availability of
contrabands "had given house wives all around the wench fever."[7]

As the prejudice in those words reveals, Northern racism could easily
turn against newly arrived contrabands, and it did. Cairo, Illinois, had many

bitterly prejudiced racists who made their feelings known. Across the North, partisan Democratic newspapers warned against a massive influx of African Americans. One Illinois paper demanded the enforcement of state laws prohibiting blacks from entering the state and warned of danger to the white laboring population. Another Illinois paper charged that the government intended to flood the state with black slaves whose competition for jobs would devastate the white working man. Its racist editor declared that Illinois had enough worthless black people. Forty thousand whites in Ohio signed a petition demanding that African Americans be kept out of the state. A Pennsylvania newspaper implausibly claimed that contrabands were infesting parts of the state like a plague of locusts; their presence, the paper claimed, would harm white laborers very severely. Even in Vermont an editor insisted that Northerners would not allow their region to become a colonization site for "uncivilized" slaves who would degrade the people of the free states.

Because these racist objections often came from areas where few African Americans lived, they indicated the wide reach of racial prejudice and fears. Secretary of State Edwin Stanton—worried about a negative impact on the fall elections—ordered a halt to the relocation of contrabands. In his annual report at the end of 1862, he tried to reassure the North that former slaves would stay in the South. Stanton asserted that black Southerners would not leave their homes in the South as long as they could be safe there. Lincoln also declared that African Americans had escaped to the North only because they had been fleeing from slavery. Republican Party newspapers repeated the same arguments, trying to defuse opposition that had flared up over the mere possibility of black migration. Obviously racial prejudices were strong. It would be a challenge to gain freedom for runaway slaves, even those who were greatly helping the Union, not to mention equal rights.

Slaves were aiding the Union and undermining the institution that oppressed them, but emancipation was not yet on the Union's agenda. Black leaders in the North wanted to put it there, despite the difficulties that lay ahead. They knew that there was much more to do, so they continued to work energetically. Their priority was freedom for almost four million African Americans in bondage. Next came two greater challenges: winning for black men the opportunity to fight, and then demanding equal rights and full citizenship for all African Americans. Freedom meant living with equal rights in the United States, not emigration or deportation elsewhere.

Black leaders kept the idea of emancipation before the public. They followed a wise strategy—they stayed *ahead* of the debate so they could move it forward. Their arguments for freedom, military service, and equal rights fit together in a logical progression. Attacking and ending slavery were essential to winning the war. Recruiting and arming black soldiers were the path to victory and preservation of the Union. Victory then should bring a chance to attack the humiliating discrimination faced by all African Americans. Demanding much more than the racist white majority was willing to contemplate, Northern black leaders argued for equality.

Freedom remained their first priority and the way to preserve the Union. James McCune Smith, a pharmacist and physician who had graduated from the University of Glasgow, argued that the only solution was immediate emancipation. He stood up to a wealthy white abolitionist who was willing to tolerate the return of contrabands; Smith insisted that there could be no compromise on freedom. From the early days of the war Frederick Douglass argued in his newspaper "*The simple way, then, to put an end to the savage and desolating war now waged by the slaveholders, is to strike down slavery itself.*" The United States should win "by 'carrying the war into Africa.' Let the slaves and free colored people be called into service, and formed into a liberating army, to march into the South and raise the banner of Emancipation."[8]

Although the army was turning away African American volunteers, Douglass urged blacks to adopt a military spirit, buy guns, and train themselves in the use of weapons. That way blacks would be ready to serve in the army as soon as the nation called on them. In time, he firmly believed, black regiments would have the chance to fight, to bring freedom to the slaves, and to advance human rights. Military service, he argued, was the way to win equal rights.

Douglass and others insisted that the man who fights for the nation would gain the right to claim America as his country and to enforce that claim. The war thus was a battle against slavery in the South and against prejudice in the North. Black leaders wanted and needed to root out that prejudice everywhere. Even in racially liberal Massachusetts, complained John Rock, blacks were barred from good employment and from all kinds of public places, such as restaurants, hotels, theaters, and even some churches. Rock emphasized that African Americans were determined to fight the Confederacy, and he believed that the nation then would have to respect the manhood of black soldiers.

The *Weekly Anglo-African* did not forget the needs of Southern blacks. "What course can be clearer" or more "just . . . [and] humane," it asked in November 1861, than to provide land to "freed men who know best how to cultivate . . . lands which they have bought and paid for by their sweat and blood?"[9] Northern black leaders thus worked for freedom, opportunity, and equal rights for all African Americans. They prodded the Congress and the president to move forward, and they did not hesitate to criticize when progress came too slowly or was temporarily turned back.

In 1862, events on the battlefield gave powerful support to their cause. Ironically, at that point it was the *lack* of progress in subduing the rebellion that aided the cause of freedom. Military reverses that depressed lawmakers encouraged the black abolitionists, who gained an opportunity to reemphasize their arguments. As the North continued to learn how difficult winning the war would be, every defeat strengthened the abolitionists' case. Because the war was going badly, first Congress and then President Lincoln decided that they had to do more. Military necessity proved to be a force that was strong enough to undermine racist opposition.

Early in 1862 there were some potentially important victories in the west. General Grant captured forts in Tennessee that would give the Union access to rivers that reached deep into Confederate territory. Admiral David Farragut captured New Orleans, the first step toward a goal of controlling the Mississippi River and cutting the Confederacy in two. But things went badly in the east. George McClellan delayed his major campaign against Richmond again and again. Meanwhile, Confederate General Stonewall Jackson ran rings around Federal forces in the Shenandoah Valley. Then, when McClellan's large army finally moved on Richmond, the huge effort was a failure, despite the fact that McClellan had superior numbers. Observers noticed that President Lincoln looked profoundly depressed. Lincoln himself said that he could not survive if his sorrow were any greater. Something had to be done. The Union had to take stronger measures against the Confederacy.

The Republican-controlled Congress seemed to learn that lesson more rapidly than President Lincoln. After prohibiting army officers from returning fugitive slaves to their masters, Congress acted against slavery in the District of Columbia, which—unlike the states—was under direct federal authority. Slaves from Maryland and Virginia were running away to the District, and slave catchers prowled the streets, creating an intolerable situation. The lawmakers approved a program of compensated emancipation in which owners would receive $300 for each slave. Almost three thousand slaves thus gained their freedom. The law also offered colonization to those freed and set aside $100,000 to assist their emigration. But colonization attracted little or no interest among black Americans.

In the spring and summer Congress went further. First the legislators passed a law prohibiting slavery in all the western territories of the United States. Then in July 1862 they passed a Second Confiscation Act. This law confiscated and freed the slaves of all disloyal masters—defining loyalty to the Confederacy in a very broad manner—and appropriated $500,000 for colonization. No longer did a slave have to be used in direct support of the rebellion—essentially all slaves in the rebellious states were covered. In addition, the Second Confiscation Act authorized the president to use slaves in the military in any manner he deemed appropriate. Of course, this law would not immediately reach most slaves because they remained under Confederate control, but it was a major advance in policy.

Republican response to these changes was positive, though not always for pure motives. The Republican governor of Iowa declared that it was time for blacks to die on the battlefield, so that the casualties were not all white. Black leaders reacted to the law with praise and criticism, lauding what was good and calling for improvements wherever Congress's actions fell short. Emancipation in the District of Columbia had been cause for rejoicing. A delighted Frederick Douglass wrote to Charles Sumner, the abolitionist senator from Massachusetts, "I trust I am not dreaming, but the events taking place seem like a dream."[10] The compensation to slaveholders was another matter. John Rock expressed the views of many when he asked, "Why talk about compensating masters? Compensate them for what? . . . It is the slave who ought to be compensated."[11] The Second Confiscation Act, despite its provisions on colonization, represented progress with even more potential, and it inspired black leaders to press forward. On the whole, they had more reason to be pleased with Congress than with President Lincoln.

Lincoln's thinking continued to lag behind the Congress. In March 1862 he renewed his ideas for gradual emancipation and colonization. He urged Congress to go on record that it would support states that adopted gradual emancipation by giving federal compensation for slaveholders. Gradual emancipation, he claimed, was better than a sudden change to freedom, and he denied any plan to interfere with slavery in the states. His idea for emancipation was merely an option, a matter of free choice, for slaveholding states. Lincoln's allies lobbied lawmakers and gave speeches, vigorously promoting federally funded colonization as part of his proposal. On both points, Congress registered its readiness to cooperate. But nothing would happen unless slaveholding states decided to emancipate. This was far less than the immediate end of slavery that African Americans desired.

While Lincoln moved slowly on policy, Southern slaves continued to show their hunger for freedom and their readiness to help the Union. Wherever the Union army established a presence, slaves defied the masters and their slave patrols in order to be free. Along the South Carolina coast thousands reached Union lines, a total of nearly ten thousand by the summer of 1862. In Louisiana, General Butler notified his superiors that runaways were numbering in the thousands every day. Many plantations along the

Gulf Coast were deserted. Slaveholders recorded their dismay in plantation journals or personal diaries. They complained of a stampede of blacks fleeing slavery. Those who remained were not obedient and were planning to make their escape as well. Some slaveholders expected to lose all their slaves. Others worried about a possible rebellion.

Union commanders—now required *not* to return runaways—were glad to have the labor of these runaway slaves. They put them to work on a large variety of tasks, which the blacks usually undertook cheerfully for their liberators. They did much heavy labor, such as building forts, throwing up ramparts, or felling trees that could be laid side by side to make a "corduroy road" that would not turn into mud. They moved ammunition, unloaded supplies, drove wagons, and cared for the huge number of horses needed by an army. Some manned boats in coastal areas or worked as cooks and butchers. The women who reached Union lines also found ways to support the soldiers, often by washing and mending clothes or by cooking and preparing baked goods for the troops. All this labor went on despite a frequent failure to pay wages or deliver promised food and shelter.

Even more important for the future was the demonstration by the "contrabands" that they could work and succeed in a system of free labor. Their energy gave the lie to the old claim by slaveholders that whipping and coercion were necessary to make a slave productive. The "contrabands" went to work along the Sea Islands of South Carolina, and soon in occupied parts of Louisiana. Their efforts to grow foodstuffs or cotton impressed federal officials. These crops aided the Union war effort and relieved the government of the financial burden of providing for them. The results were so encouraging that they disproved the racist ideology of slaveholders. From South Carolina Special Agent Edward Pierce reported to the secretary of the treasury that the stereotype of lazy slaves was false. He had seen them working hard and persistently. He was convinced that with the incentives of a system of free labor former slaves would be as productive as any other race.

A captain in the Union army made a similar report to his superiors. He had never seen a contraband refuse work as long as he knew he would receive a reasonable wage, or even moderate wages. On Ladies Island, South Carolina, the superintendent of a plantation agreed that former slaves could adapt to the system of free labor, with its incentives. He testified that in freedom blacks were working harder, more thoroughly, and with more energy than had been the case under the discouraging conditions of slavery. This evidence of productive labor was significant. As one Union officer put it, these facts exploded the old dogma that African Americans made good slaves but were worthless and helpless when free.

Such evidence supported African Americans' claims to economic opportunity and equal rights as citizens. Some Northern newspapers reported that the contrabands were proving their ability to support themselves in freedom. These papers reported that their industry and intelligence were satisfactory and concluded that former slaves would do well when provided with incentives. Countering the prevalent racism, some Republicans were now beginning to argue for acceptance and inclusion of freed slaves in American society, rather than colonization.

Racist objections were hard to overcome, however, and partisan politics raised additional barriers. Newspapers loyal to the Democratic Party routinely ignored the Republicans' evidence or evidence from any source. They simply refused to print evidence of black industry and productivity. Instead, they invented arguments that would serve their partisan interests. Loudly and routinely Democratic newspapers claimed that the government was maintaining lazy, useless contrabands, at huge cost to the taxpayer and with accompanying risks to the future of white laborers.

But slaves and contrabands were not merely working. They also were showing how they could help win the war. In May 1862 another slave stole a ship, this time from Charleston, South Carolina, the very city where secession and the war had begun. The ship was the *Planter*, a Confederate sidewheel steamer that carried ammunition and artillery. The thief was Robert Smalls, assistant pilot of the *Planter*, a slave whose owner had hired him out to the Confederacy. In the middle of a dark night, after white officers had gone ashore, Smalls and several black crewmen quietly cast off from their dock. Then they picked up family members and boldly sailed past several Confederate outposts, giving the proper signals and arousing no suspicion. Outside the harbor, by raising a bed sheet as a white flag, they were able safely to deliver the *Planter* to the surrounding Union fleet. A jubilant Smalls announced to a Federal officer that he was returning some of the United States' guns.

The Union general in overall command along South Carolina's coast was David Hunter. He had already become convinced that blacks could help the war effort, and he now decided it was time to issue an emancipation proclamation and raise black troops. Hunter alerted the secretary of war to his plans, and then went ahead. But when the general published his emancipation decree, Lincoln swiftly overruled him, just as he had overruled Frémont in Missouri.

Again the president had disappointed black leaders, white abolitionists, and the more strongly antislavery wing of his own party. Free black spokesmen were quick to criticize and put pressure on the president. Philip A. Bell, editor of the black newspaper the *Pacific Appeal,* in San Francisco, called Lincoln's action a proslavery proclamation. It raised doubts about the president's willingness to act against slavery and encouraged the rebels who were trying to destroy the Union. An angry Frederick Douglass charged that Lincoln was planning to restore the union on the old basis of a corrupt compromise with slavery, which would allow slaveholders to retain their power and encourage them to seek more.

Under pressure from the war and these abolitionists, however, Lincoln's views were starting to evolve. When he voided Frémont's proclamation, Lincoln had said that confiscating and liberating slaves could not be justified under military law but should be left to lawmakers. Nine months later he took a very different stand. When he overruled Hunter's emancipation decree, Lincoln now suggested that as president and commander-in-chief he could decide that such a step had become necessary to maintain the government.

Still Lincoln hung back from declaring freedom or taking strong action under the Second Confiscation Act. Instead he urged the four slaveholding states that remained in the Union to adopt his plan of voluntary, gradual emancipation with Federal compensation. He made a special effort to convince the congressmen from the border states. Using all his tact and diplomacy, Lincoln argued that gradual emancipation could help win the war while giving slaveholders some benefit from an institution that was being undermined every day. He also suggested there was cheap land available in South America to resettle freed slaves abroad. His efforts were in vain. The border state congressmen refused to act and bluntly told him to stay out of their affairs.

Next Lincoln scheduled a meeting with several black leaders from Washington, D.C. In this widely reported meeting he argued strongly for colonization. It was not one of the president's best moments. Urging these native-born Americans to immigrate to Central America, he observed that nowhere in the nation were black people treated as equals. Then he deplored the fact that because there were two races in the country, white men were killing each other. Saying that there would be no war except for the presence of black people in America, he seemed to blame African Americans for the conflict. Then he told these individuals that if they failed to lead an emigration movement, they would be acting in an extremely selfish way. It was their responsibility to help others who were less fortunate—by leaving the country.

African Americans overwhelmingly rejected colonization or emigration. George Vashon, an attorney and educator from Pittsburgh, promptly wrote to the president. Vashon corrected Lincoln on the cause of the war—rather than being the fault of African Americans, it was the result of the racial injustices caused by whites. Vashon regretted that the president's remarks would tend to inflame racist attitudes. Robert Purvis (a wealthy man of mixed race who identified as black) insisted that "this is our country as much as it is yours, and we will not leave it." Frederick Douglass lamented that Lincoln had shown "his contempt for negroes." How deplorable, Douglass wrote, that the president had endorsed racial prejudice and hatred.[12]

But the lack of progress in the war and the arguments of black and white abolitionists were influencing Lincoln's plans. In July he admitted, after overruling General Hunter, that his policies were unpopular with some Republicans whose support he could not afford to lose. Just before Congress passed the Second Confiscation Act, he had shared with two members of his cabinet a measure that he was privately considering. He had given a lot of thought, he revealed, to the possibility of issuing an emancipation proclamation. In fact, he had almost concluded that it was a military necessity. The Union had to be preserved, and Lincoln was becoming convinced that the North had to free the slaves or suffer defeat.

Soon Lincoln revealed his intentions to the whole cabinet. By this time its members shared Lincoln's sense of crisis and did not object on principle. But they advised the president to wait until the Union army won a victory. In this way his proclamation would not appear to be the desperate act of a nation on the road to defeat.

A sufficiently important victory arrived in the fall. In September Confederate General Robert E. Lee invaded Maryland and fought Union forces under General McClellan at Antietam Creek, near the town of Sharpsburg. The Battle of Antietam was extremely bloody and less than a crushing victory. But McClellan's army stopped Lee and forced him to retreat. The time for Lincoln's proclamation had arrived.

On September 22, 1862, Lincoln issued a Preliminary Emancipation Proclamation (which Democrats denounced as unconstitutional). He repeated that the purpose of the war was to preserve the Union—to restore the normal constitutional relation between the United States and those states in rebellion. He then put forward two plans that would lead to the end of slavery. The first was a continuation of proposals he had made previously. The second broke new ground.

Lincoln first promised that he would recommend to Congress his idea of gradual, or immediate, compensated emancipation. This plan involved slaveholding states taking a voluntary step on a schedule they determined, with financial compensation from the federal government. It would be available to all states that were not in rebellion, and it would include efforts to colonize African Americans outside the United States. He promised that more details on this proposal would be forthcoming in December, when Congress reconvened.

The second part of the Preliminary Emancipation Proclamation was new. Lincoln now gave notice that on January 1, 1863, he would name all the states or parts of states that were then in rebellion. All the slaves in those areas would, from that date forward, be forever free, and the armed forces of the United States would protect and maintain their freedom. Here—at last, to the delight of black leaders—was a measure of military emancipation that would not be overruled.

Lincoln had taken a great step forward toward freedom, but he was still being careful on the issue of slaveholders' rights. How would the list of states in rebellion be determined? The proclamation gave a clear answer. Any state that on January 1 was in good faith represented in Congress, by representatives chosen in elections in which a majority of the voters had participated, would *not* be considered as in rebellion. Thus the seceded states had an opportunity to avoid emancipation. They had one hundred days in which they could reconsider their rebellion, elect representatives to Congress, and keep their slaves. The four slaveholding border states that had never left the Union would not, of course, be covered by the proclamation. Slavery would remain in force there. The Preliminary Proclamation took note of some of Congress's previous antislavery legislation and closed by promising to recommend compensation for any loyal person who lived in a rebel area and had lost his or her slaves.

Frederick Douglass did not hesitate to express his excitement over the Preliminary Emancipation Proclamation. "We shout for joy that we live to record this righteous decree," he editorialized in his newspaper. At last, he thought, the paralyzing influence of the slaveholding border states had failed to control policy, and he assured loyal men that "with freedom to the slave will come peace and safety to your country."[13] Other black leaders were more restrained. They knew that the societal racism that had made Lincoln so slow to act had not disappeared. And just as Lincoln worried about the political cost of his proclamation, they worried that something might derail his plan before January 1.

In December, as promised, Lincoln urged Congress to adopt gradual, compensated emancipation and colonization. He did so in the form of three proposed constitutional amendments. The first would give slaveholding states until 1900 to end slavery with the benefit of federal compensation. Their payment would be U.S. bonds delivered in installments, or at one time, depending on whether they emancipated in stages or on a certain date.

The second proposal would add to the Constitution a declaration that any slave who actually became free through the events of war would be forever free. Slave owners who had not been disloyal would be compensated for such slaves. The third proposed amendment specifically gave Congress authority to appropriate money for colonization of African Americans outside the United States. In a striking sign of Lincoln's continuing gestures of deference to slaveholding states, the first of these proposals included a provision that any state that emancipated but later decided to reintroduce slavery would simply have to repay the bonds it had received.

There are indications that Lincoln really hoped that some of the rebellious states in the Confederacy might return to the Union and keep their slaves. Not only did his proclamation make that possible, but he also sent allies into the South to encourage Southerners to hold elections, even if *fewer* than half the voters participated. Yet even if the rebels ignored his offer, Lincoln could benefit politically. By giving rebellious states an opportunity to return to the Union, he made it possible for his supporters to argue that Confederates bore the responsibility for emancipation. By refusing to return to the Union, *they* had caused emancipation. On the subject of colonization, there is no reason to doubt Lincoln's interest. In December and January he pursued a colonization plan that in the spring of 1863 actually sent hundreds of individuals to an island off Haiti.

As the end of 1862 neared, free blacks throughout the North waited anxiously for word about the final proclamation. In the contraband camps near Washington, escaped slaves started a tradition known as "Watch Night" by staying up late and watching for the arrival at midnight of January 1. "We shall be free in jus' about five minutes," cried one man.[14] Another, whom slavery had torn from his family, rejoiced that "dey can't sell my wife and child any more, bless de Lord!"[15] On January 1 Lincoln was busy for much of the day with a traditional New Year's reception in the White House. But finally, well into the evening, Lincoln slipped away from the reception, steadied his hand, and signed the proclamation. His declaration of freedom included a statement that black men would be received into the armed forces, at least to garrison forts, and serve on ships. Military service by African Americans would begin.

By word of mouth, special newspaper editions, and the telegraph, the news spread quickly. Relief and joy were the dominant reactions among free blacks. "Great processions of colored and white men marched to and fro and passed in front of the White House and congratulated President Lincoln on his proclamation," recalled Henry McNeil Turner, a prominent AME minister. "Nothing like it will ever be seen again in this life."[16] Frederick

Douglass declared that emancipation was the greatest event in the history of the United States. January first, a day when the "hiring out" of slaves to work for someone other than the master had separated many families, now became a day of rejoicing.

Still, the leaders of the black community in the North knew that their work was far from over. The AME's *Christian Recorder* noted that the proclamation applied only to slaves in the Confederacy and that the border states, and even some rebel areas, were excepted. The newspaper was right. Lincoln's proclamation did not cover the border states still in the Union, nor did it apply to large parts of Virginia and Louisiana where Federal troops were in control. Lincoln also omitted Tennessee because the wartime governor he had appointed there did not want to enrage slaveholders.

Robert Hamilton, editor of the *Weekly Anglo-African*, made another important point. The proclamation was only a war measure. Lincoln had in fact justified his proclamation as a necessary war measure issued under his authority as commander-in-chief in time of an actual rebellion. To Hamilton this meant it had no more humanitarian content than the firing of a cannon. Blacks in Harrisburg, Pennsylvania, were more conflicted—they acknowledged that it was a war measure, but they saw in it the influence of God. Both had identified an important and troubling point. The legal standing of a war measure could be questioned once the war was over. Soon newspapers and commentators throughout the North would point out that greater legal certainty—such as a constitutional amendment—would be necessary to destroy slavery.

The specter of colonization also remained alive. As long as Lincoln pursued the idea of removing African Americans from their country, and as long as white citizens rejected the idea of living with free black Americans, equal rights were impossible. Even in the joyous aftermath of the Emancipation Proclamation, black Northerners protested against colonization. Blacks held a mass meeting in Queens County, New York, and declared that the United States was their native country. A black writer from New Jersey asked the president why African Americans had less right to a home in the United States than did Lincoln himself. In Philadelphia a meeting of African Americans declared, "Shall we . . . leave our homes, forsake our birth-place, and flee to a strange land to appease the anger and prejudice of the traitors now in arms against the Government?"[17]

The war was not over, freedom was not surely won, and a long battle for equal rights lay ahead. But how much had been accomplished! The Emancipation Proclamation was now a reality, and exciting changes were under way. Blacks could feel that they had put freedom on the nation's agenda. Tens of thousands of slaves in the Confederacy had escaped from their masters. Thousands more were eagerly watching for their chance to become free, and in the North black abolitionists were not daunted. On January 8, 1863, H. Ford Douglas, who had already managed to enlist in an army unit, argued that the current of events was on their side. "The war," he said, "will educate Mr. Lincoln out of his idea of the deportation of the Negro, quite as fast as it has some of his other proslavery ideas with respect to employing them as soldiers."[18]

For now, however, the Union army was only beginning to penetrate more deeply into Southern rebel territory. The South held almost four million slaves, and for the large majority of them, freedom was still a dream. Everything depended on Union military success. In the meantime, bondage and the Confederacy were oppressive realities.

Notes

1. Quoted in Mary Beth Norton, David M. Katzman, Paul D. Escott, Howard P. Chudacoff, Thomas G. Paterson, and William M. Tuttle Jr., *A People and a Nation: A History of the United States*, fifth edition (Boston: Houghton Mifflin Company, 1998), 393.

2. Quoted in David Williams, *I Freed Myself: African American Self-Emancipation in the Civil War Era* (New York: Cambridge University Press, 2014), 19.

3. Quoted in James M. McPherson, *The Negro's Civil War* (New York: Ballantine Books, 1965, 1982, 1991), 27.

4. Quoted in McPherson, *The Negro's Civil War*, 17.

5. Ibid., 41, 38, 19, 164.

6. Ibid., 83.

7. Quoted in Leslie A. Schwalm, "Between Slavery and Freedom," in LeeAnn Whites and Alecia P. Long, *Occupied Women: Gender, Military Occupation, and the American Civil War* (Baton Rouge: Louisiana State University Press, 2009), 150.

8. Quoted in McPherson, *The Negro's Civil War*, 38, and in Waldo Martin, *The Mind of Frederick Douglass* (Chapel Hill: University of North Carolina Press, 1984), 60.

9. Quoted in McPherson, *The Negro's Civil War*, 297–98.

10. Ibid., 44.

11. Ibid., 44, 298.

12. Ibid, 97–98, 94.

13. Ibid., 49.

14. Ibid., 63.

15. Ibid., 63.

16. Ibid., 50.

17. Quoted in Williams, *I Freed Myself*, 111.

18. Quoted in C. Peter Ripley, ed., *The Black Abolitionist Papers*, five volumes (Chapel Hill: University of North Carolina Press, 1992), V: 166–67.

CHAPTER TWO

~

Forced to Serve the South, Desiring Freedom

Freedom for almost four million slaves depended on a Union victory. The same was true for almost 133,000 "free" blacks in the Confederacy, who had few rights and little freedom. Until that victory arrived, African Americans in the rebelling South had to live with slaveholders in a Confederate government bent on independence. Except around the margins of the Confederacy, where Union troops gradually extended their footholds, most slaves remained under Southern control, too far from the North to escape to freedom. Approximately 85 percent of the Confederacy's slaves remained in bondage throughout the war. They yearned for freedom, but they could not grasp it.

Surviving in the Confederacy was not easy. In fact, in some ways the slaves' lives became harder, as worried whites tried to intensify their control. The Southern government also saw blacks as a vital source of labor. Not only could they grow food while white men fought, but their skills and coerced labor could directly support the South's war effort. Tens of thousands had to work for the army or Confederate agencies, often in dangerous settings or unhealthy conditions. Nancy Johnson, a slave in Georgia, recalled that the rebels made her work hard for them until the war's last day. The war years brought new sources of tension, sickness, injury, and disruption of families.

But that could not eradicate hope or the will to help the North and gain their freedom. The slaves were forced to serve the South, but they did so unwillingly, and their desire for freedom undermined the Confederate war effort in a variety of ways. As the Union army made gains against the South, discipline on plantations and farms broke down. Slaves became less valuable for the South, while increasingly they found ways to help the Yankees. In an environment made more complicated by the war, the Confederacy's slaves, through their own actions, advanced the agenda of freedom.

There was no disguising the unending hardships of slavery. A British traveler in the Confederacy noted that the slaves everywhere had a sad and dejected appearance. Although blacks on a plantation he visited seemed well fed and clothed, there was no mistaking their depressed manner. A Northerner whose regiment occupied part of Louisiana agreed. He concluded that the South's slaves were not a happy people. The gloom that followed them was the product of white efforts to crush them, and it seemed that the chains of slavery weighed on their hearts.

But their suffering could not extinguish the desire for freedom. The Northern soldier asked one man if he would like to be free. Before replying, this slave looked at him searchingly. Then, after concluding that his questioner was friendly, the slave declared that "all of us would *like* to be free; but we don't see the way yet."[1] Nevertheless, many of the South's slaves had faith that freedom would come. Years later a former slave recalled, "I thought it was foolishness then, but the old time folks always felt they was to be free."[2] Even those who had a relatively good master, said another, wanted to be free and shared their hopes in the slave quarters. There "everybody talked about freedom,"[3] and sometimes they would sing and pray. "Some day this yoke's going to be lifted off our shoulders," believed one slave.[4] Her words were typical of "the whisperings among the slaves—their talking of the possibility of freedom."[5]

In the first two years of the war, before the Emancipation Proclamation was issued, slaves had only their hopes to rely on. During that time they learned that Confederate officials were determined to use black labor to aid the rebel war effort. White Southerners were confident that slavery would prove to be an advantage for them. Secessionists claimed that slaves could stay on their farms and plantations growing food, while white men went off to fight and win battles. Slaves would keep the home front productive while white men whipped the Yankees.

But this was an overestimate of both the South's resources and the slaves' devotion. Confederates quickly found that the military needed far more laborers and skilled men and women than were readily available, so they turned to slaves to fill the gap. At the same time they worried that, with many white men in the army, the plantations were not secure. Any resistance by slaves on the plantations also would increase the looming shortage of resources. Thus, slaves had a pivotal role in the Confederacy. Whether in army camps or on plantations, their cooperation or resistance became very important.

Right away, white Confederates intensified their efforts to keep the slaves under control. Fear of possible uprisings had always contradicted their claims that slavery was a warm, paternalistic relationship. Now, at the beginning of the war, governors talked of "self-preservation" and "home defense," as they organized armed companies to police slaves on the home front. The governor of Louisiana, for example, held on to thousands of weapons that had been seized from a Federal arsenal. He even sent seven thousand guns to Mississippi's governor, rather than to Confederate officials, so that both states could keep their slaves under strict supervision.

Local officials joined in the effort to keep close watch on the slaves. Young boys, or older men who were not going into the army, had to ride the roads at night, to keep the slaves in subjection. One county in North Carolina purchased a pack of dogs to help its patrollers. In Georgia some county officials hired men to serve on new, extra patrols, and Confederate soldiers sometimes helped to monitor the slaves. When the Confederate government turned to a military draft, only one year into the war, slaveholding families everywhere demanded help in policing the slaves. The Confederate Congress approved a law allowing anyone who managed twenty slaves to stay at home, enforcing order on the home front. On numerous occasions army generals also sent troops into Southern neighborhoods to prevent escapes, keep slaves under control, and make whites feel more secure. Plantation laborers were under surveillance.

Some slaveholders, usually the wealthy, ordered certain slaves to accompany them into the army. These men, called "body servants," had to work at all the necessary chores a white soldier wanted to avoid. They gathered wood for campfires, cooked meals for their masters, washed clothes, ran errands, and did whatever else was required. When Union soldiers saw these African Americans with Confederate forces, they sent word back home, and Northern newspapers reported how slavery was helping the rebel war effort. Occasionally, in the midst of battle, some of these slaves actually fired a gun. But some just wanted a chance to escape, and occasionally they succeeded.

Body servants were a small part of all the slaves near Confederate armies. A far larger number were exploited for their labor, and the government was quick to ask slaveholders for their help. Early in the war many masters, feeling an initial surge of Confederate patriotism, offered to lend their slaves to the army. They understood that the slaves' labor could help build forts and entrenchments, transport supplies, or tend to the horses and mules. But there were never enough slaves to do all the work, and the government's requests kept coming.

As time passed, slave owners became more reluctant to turn over control of their slaves, protesting abuse of their valuable "property." As early as

November 1862 one Confederate commander complained that slaveholders were no longer willing to lend their slaves to do military labor. Eventually they refused to do so, and the secretary of war admitted that voluntary cooperation by slave owners had ended. Two states, Virginia and North Carolina, complained of mistreatment of impressed slaves and pressured the Confederate government to pay a monthly wage to the slaves' masters and full compensation for those who were injured, died, or escaped. To gain slave labor, the Confederacy had to turn to other measures.

"Impressment" was the taking of anything needed by the army. Throughout the war, whenever military supplies ran short, Confederate armies took food, wagons, or other supplies from nearby farmers. Slaves were even more important. Not until 1863 did the Southern Congress pass a general law to govern all types of impressment and promise eventual repayment. But early on, local laws authorized and regulated the impressment of slaves in at least seven states. The Confederacy also claimed the labor of many free blacks, by conscripting them to work. The army's calls for black labor were especially frequent in Virginia, North Carolina, and other areas close to the scene of military conflict. Slave owners wanted to limit the number of their slaves who would be called to work and the length of time they would serve. Nevertheless, in Virginia as many as 20 percent or 25 percent of the slaves had to work directly for the Confederacy. Authorities in Virginia made at least eight calls, under the impressment system, for slaves to work on fortifications. Despite growing opposition from slave owners, the army got nearly 29,300 laborers for two-month labor terms. In North Carolina the percentage of slaves who worked for the Confederacy was closer to 10 percent.

Slaves impressed by the army faced hard, even brutally demanding labor. They did the heavy "fatigue labor," such as moving cannon, armaments, or building materials. Often they worked under pressure and in dangerous situations, close to the battlefield. Some cut down trees, built stockades, or shaped lumber for construction. The Engineer Department put many thousands to work creating entrenchments around Confederate positions. These defensive trenches had to be dug six feet deep, and their packed-earth embankment walls had to be at least two feet wide and two feet high above the trench. Slaves did this back-breaking work in gangs of three. One man swung his pick to loosen the ground, and two others came behind him to throw the dirt up and to the side with their shovels. Each team had to move approximately eight tons of earth in a day.

Such work was much harder than agricultural labor, and often it had to be done in winter, in the rain, or on swampy ground. Frequently slaves worked in water up to their waists. If they had shelter after a day of hard labor, it usually was nothing better than old tents. Often they were unable to build fires to warm themselves or dry their clothes. Injuries and sickness were common. In addition to heavy and exhausting labor, the food was poor. Sometimes the only meat that slaves had to eat was literally rotten. Under such conditions mortality rates were high, and the medical care furnished by the Confederacy was totally inadequate. Even Confederate officers complained about the slaves' treatment. At one point the editor of the *Richmond Examiner* decided to investigate. After visiting an Engineer Hospital in that city he reported that slaves were dying off like penned-up animals. In Georgia, a prominent minister and planter lost four out of seven slaves that had been taken to work for the army. Sickness, death, and injuries to impressed slaves were common.

While large numbers of slaves were victims of impressment, some Confederate bureaus and offices actually hired thousands of slaves, especially in Virginia, to perform a great variety of important tasks. "Hiring out" was not a new system. For years Virginia's slave owners had been hiring out slaves whose labor they did not need on plantations. When the slaves did work for someone else, most or all of their wages had to be turned over to the owner. Skilled urban artisans had often worked under this system, and now the

From the start of the war, white Confederates tried to exploit black labor in support of the war effort. These slaves were mounting cannon to attack Fort Sumter. Library of Congress, Prints and Photographs Division.

Confederacy turned to hiring slaves on a large scale. Under the hiring system many additional thousands worked for the Quartermaster Department, the Confederate States Ambulance Shop, the Petersburg Wagon Shop, Confederate gun shops, the Commissary Department, the Navy Department, the Richmond Ordnance Bureau, the Tredegar Iron Works, or other agencies.

Slaves often did skilled work for Confederate departments or bureaus, but their lives were not easy. Sometimes their tasks were dangerous and disgusting as well. In the Commissary Department, slaves did the bloody work of carving up animals in its slaughterhouses. Blacks dug tunnels in the earth and worked in mines in southwest Virginia. For the Niter and Mining Bureau, slaves mined niter used in the manufacture of gunpowder. They also mined salt and iron for the war effort. Some slaves had to prepare artificial niter beds two feet deep and four feet wide. Into these niter beds went carcasses, animal refuse of all kinds, decaying vegetable matter, and putrid water and liquid waste. Then they had to stir these stinking, decomposing beds. By the end of 1864, the Richmond area had 265,000 cubic feet of niter beds, the most in the Confederacy. In one county three-quarters of the male slaves worked making niter, salt, or iron.

Many of those slaves who were skilled workers worked long hours in a great variety of shops and settings. Hundreds of boatmen worked for the Quartermaster Department, ferrying supplies by water. Their boats typically had a few white officers in charge of a large number of black crewmen. The Tredegar Iron Works had a canal fleet manned by forty-two black crewmen and only nine white officers. Richmond's Ambulance Shop employed seven slave blacksmiths and one wheelwright, all of whom worked from 4:30 a.m. to 8:00 p.m. In the Petersburg Wagon Shop one hundred skilled slaves worked in various trades—harness maker, blacksmith, carpenter, wagon maker, painter, farrier, wheelwright, and bricklayer. Almost another hundred were hostlers, sawyers, stock drivers, teamsters, and yard hands. Caring for animals was a huge task, as General Robert E. Lee's army required seven thousand horses and fourteen thousand mules every fifteen months. Slaves did most of the work, whether baling forage or feeding and caring for these animals.

In the Navy Department, where there was always a labor shortage, African Americans worked as machinists, carpenters, boilermakers, firemen, molders, and shop hands. Other jobs there included axmen, sawyers, cooks, caulkers, joiners, bricklayers, and boat hands. In the iron industry hundreds of slaves and free blacks provided not only muscle, but skill. In the Tredegar Iron Works, which was the Confederacy's largest industrial factory, 1,200 blacks worked as iron puddlers, bricklayers, painters, packers, blacksmiths, or teamsters. In the Ordnance Bureau, blacks manufactured heavy guns, artillery, and ammunition; two thousand African Americans worked in factories spread over five southeastern states. Some smelted lead and made bullets. Thousands of slaves also worked building or repairing railroads for the Confederacy. In Virginia more than three thousand repaired the roads, worked at depots, or labored as firemen, cleaners, train hands, carpenters, blacksmiths, or in the machine shop. Most bridges constructed in the South during the war were built by black laborers.

With the war producing thousands of injured soldiers, African Americans became the mainstay of many hospitals in the Confederacy. Richmond alone had six hospitals. The most successful of these, known as Chimborazo Hospital, could not have operated without the work of 256 black nurses and cooks employed to care for nearly 4,000 sick and wounded. Men and some women served as hospital attendants and nurses, though men were preferable because they were better able to lift patients. Slave women usually served as cooks and laundresses. In Richmond, Virginia, slaves made up more than three-quarters of the nurses. After major battles thousands of wounded soldiers arrived at Richmond's hospitals, which often hired additional slaves to help in the emergency. Medical care for black workers, however, was a different matter. Hospitals for sick or injured slaves in government service were poorly managed, and many patients died.

The government's demand for slave labor was so great that in Virginia it monopolized the hiring market for male slaves. Some agencies, such as the Tredegar Iron Works, actually purchased slaves from their masters in order to secure their supply of skilled laborers. But industrial production competed with agricultural efforts. Every slave who left a farm or plantation to work in the military or Confederate bureaus was one less worker who could grow food. And with most white men conscripted or volunteering in the armies, daily life and routines in the rural South began to change substantially.

For the majority of slaves who did not leave their plantations and farms, the war created a new opportunity to modify the conditions of life and lighten the burdens of bondage. There had always been an ongoing struggle of wills, with opposed strategies and aims, between the masters and the slaves. Now the daily contest of wills became more emotionally charged. While concerned whites tried to tighten their control, African Americans looked for ways to improve their situation. This intensifying contest between slave and master, between black and white, was the reality on plantations and farms during the Civil War. Eventually, as the war dragged on, African Americans gained more ground.

Slaves knew about the controversies between North and South, and that knowledge raised their hopes and their determination to seek freedom. The simple meaning of the war was that the Union and the Confederacy were "fightin' over us [blacks]."[6] Susie King Taylor from Georgia heard her parents say "the Yankee was going to set all the slaves free." Consequently, she "wanted to see these wonderful 'Yankees' so much. . . . Oh. How those people prayed for freedom."[7] On one plantation the slaves were so encouraged that they "'clared to Marse Tom [that] they ain't gwine to be no more beatin's."[8] A Louisiana slaveholder lamented that his house servants had become lazy and disobedient—the excitement of possible freedom had infected them. Other unhappy slave owners sensed that their slaves were taking advantage of the war, feeling independent, and changing as the political world changed.

Because most slaves were too far away from Union lines to escape to freedom, gaining greater influence or latitude on the plantation was their immediate goal and best alternative. Instinctively they moved to exploit every little advantage. Plantation mistresses felt this change very early. When their husbands joined the army, these women found themselves confronting new challenges and having to act in new and unaccustomed roles. It was neither easy nor pleasant for them, as the slaves soon began to undermine the mistresses' authority.

On a Virginia plantation the slaves' behavior immediately showed one mistress that life would be different with her husband away. The slaves' behavior told her that they considered her a usurper with no legitimate authority over them. Similarly, a South Carolina woman complained that the slaves disregarded her orders more and more each day. In Mississippi one woman admitted that she lacked the courage to dominate her slaves, and other women admitted that "managing negroes" was beyond their abilities. Increasingly the slaves began to challenge prewar rules and assert themselves more. Some women wrote to their husbands in the army, lamenting that the slaves would not "mind" them. But even men who were able to stay at home found that their slaves were insubordinate and refused to work as they had before. With slaves so "demoralized," it was no surprise that the women had trouble.

Whipping, the essential element of the coercion that made slavery possible, was a major concern for slaves during the war. It loomed large both for slaves and plantation mistresses. A slave woman in Tennessee announced that she was no longer going to be whipped. Her announcement was not unusual, for all slaves wanted to banish the lash. When blacks belonging to one white woman slowed their work in the fields, she sensed that in anticipation of gaining freedom from the Yankees they also would resist a whipping. Before long this woman was negotiating with one of her slaves, promising him that he would not get another lick if he would be humble and submissive.

The problem was not just that white women were unaccustomed to whipping slaves. They also feared retaliation from the supposedly "loyal" and affectionate slaves. Many worried anxiously about a slave revolt, since many white men were away. Fear and rumors spread among women who said they felt defenseless. A woman in Virginia admitted that her fear of the Yankees was nothing compared to her fear of a possible slave uprising. Consequently, many were actually afraid to use the whip.

These experiences frightened and embittered slave-owning women, but they also gave some of them new insight about the realities of the South's "peculiar institution"—slavery. In frustration a Tennessee mistress decided that she and others would be better off once slavery was ended. Others said that they were sick of trying to manage slaves, and the wife of a South Carolina congressman told her husband that she could not handle slaves who thought they were free. Slaves could not be trusted, concluded another woman, who complained that for money any of them would quickly betray their white owners. Virginia's Judith McGuire realized the truth—it was natural for men and women to want to be free.

That desire caused slaves to escape into Union lines whenever possible. Wherever Northern troops advanced into rebel areas, slaves fled from their plantations. Even impressed slaves, who were supposedly under the control of the Confederate army, showed that they could not be stopped. If they were digging entrenchments for the army, that meant they were near the front lines and close to the safety of Union-held territory. One Confederate officer explained why progress on his fortifications was slow. His labor force was dissolving before his eyes—most of his slaves had run away. Slaveholders in areas near the Union army's operations constantly worried that even a rumor of invasion or slave impressment would set off a wave of escapes from their counties. One historian has estimated that almost 38,000 African Americans fled to freedom from Confederate areas in Virginia during the Civil War. Caroline County, in the northeastern part of the state, started the war with 1,889 adult male slaves. By the end of 1864 only 225 remained. Half of the slaves in nearby Hanover County escaped during the war. Eventually almost 500,000 slaves made it to freedom during the war.

White men in positions of authority tried to crack down on runaways and slave "insubordination." Assuming that harsher punishments could have a deterrent effect, they treated slaves who ran away with brutality. Aaron Mitchell ran toward Union lines in Missouri with another slave from his plantation named Alfred. Unfortunately, both were caught, and Mitchell was taken back to his owner and whipped. The other man was not so lucky. "Just before we got to the house," Mitchell recalled, "I heard a pistol fired. . . . When I got there,

Slaves building fortifications for the Confederacy, 1863. Courtesy of "The Civil War in America from the *Illustrated London News*": a joint project by Sandra J. Still, Emily E. Katt, Collection Management, and the Beck Center of Emory University.

I saw Alfred lying in a little ice house in the yard. He was dead. He had been Shot through the heart."[9] Escaped slave Archy Vaughn told a gruesome story. He was caught before he could get into Federal lines, and his owner then took him to an isolated spot, tied him up, and with a knife castrated him and cut off the top of one ear.

Families of runaways also faced special white hostility. When a slave managed to get away successfully, often his wife or his parents left behind suffered at the hands of an infuriated owner. Patsey Leach's husband reached Union lines, but then the owner came to Patsey's cabin and "knocked me to the floor senseless . . . When I recovered my sense he beat me with a cowhide." The beatings resumed later until "I could not wear my underclothes without their becoming saturated in blood."[10] A slave woman in Missouri wrote to her husband, who had joined the U.S. Army, and said that she had experienced nothing but trouble since he left. Her owners abused and beat her and quarreled with her constantly because he had joined the Yankees.

Often slaves who made it to Union lines tried to slip back and lead their loved ones to safety. Whites became especially determined to stop these "missionaries" from freeing additional slaves. When Confederate army officers caught "missionaries," they reacted by convening drumhead court-martials and hanging the "guilty" on the spot. But they had to be always on their guard, because slaves who gained their freedom tried to help others. A Northern officer reported that slaves who had traveled hundreds of miles to gain their freedom were determined to go back and help others. "'I am going for my family,' they say. 'Are you not afraid to risk it?' 'No, I know the way.' Colored men will help colored men and they will work along the by paths and get through." [11] Once the Union began accepting runaway slaves into its army, these black soldiers mounted individual and organized efforts to free others. For example, in August 1863 four black soldiers from a Louisiana unit went into St. Bernard Parish, seized horses, mules, and carts, and liberated seventy-five slaves from bondage.

To hold on to their slaves, some owners adopted a different strategy—they removed their "property" to a safer location deeper in the Confederacy. For example, one morning the slaves on a large plantation in eastern North Carolina found themselves surrounded by armed soldiers. They had to get into wagons and ended up on land their owner had rented far away from Union forces. In the deep South some owners thought they would be safer in Texas, where large-scale military operations were less common. Therefore, as ex-slaves recalled, many slaveholders started moving their "property" to the west, hoping that in Texas there would never be freedom. These removals tore many families apart, as slaves often had a husband, wife, or child on a neighboring plantation. The slaves resisted by showing an increased determination to escape to the Yankees. When Confederate officials urged a Mississippi planter to move his slaves to a safer location, he responded that every black person on his place would run to the Yankees before accepting a relocation.

Once Lincoln issued his Emancipation Proclamations, the determination of slaves to resist and to change their daily routines grew. There was no keeping this news from the slaves. The whites themselves were the source of much information, as they energetically discussed and debated events among themselves. One slave remembered listening to his owners as they read their newspapers and talked over dinner. Another woman who had managed to learn to read would steal the newspapers and share information on the war with her fellow slaves. When one black woman saw her mistress crying over the deaths of Confederate soldiers, she concluded that the mistress was crying from fear that her slaves were going to be set free.

Blacks showed great initiative in gathering and spreading the news about the war. As early as May 1861 planters began to marvel about the fact that slaves seemed well informed about everything that was happening. A Louisiana slaveholder complained that his slaves knew more about politics than most white men. In Florida, complained a Confederate general, slaves carried the news of emancipation through the swamps at night, and he could not stop it. A slave in Mississippi worked as a runner, taking news about freedom to all the nearby plantations. What was called the "slave grapevine" worked remarkably well. A captured Confederate admitted that one of his slaves told him about the proclamation a full five days before any other mention of it reached him. He was not the only white Southerner who first heard about Lincoln's proclamation from his slaves.

News of the Emancipation Proclamation brought joy, hope, and excitement to the slaves. On many farms they gathered together at night to talk about the proclamation and think about the meaning of freedom. "We're free—no more whippings and beating," cried one man.[12] "We're free now, bless de Lord!" said another. "They can't sell my wife and child any more, bless de Lord! No more that! No more that!"[13] One woman made up an impromptu song. Its chorus repeated the joyous news that there was no more selling, no more hiring, and no more whipping today. The time to celebrate freedom had come. Another woman, a grandmother who had been hired out away from her home, dropped her hoe when she heard about the proclamation. She ran several miles back to her mistress's plantation, where she confronted the woman, looked at her "real hard," and yelled "I'm free! Yes, I'm free."[14]

As happy as the slaves were, their owners were often just as angry. In Norfolk, Virginia, the slaveholders took out their frustration on the slaves, mistreating them and telling them that no one on earth had the power to free them. Blacks in that area had so many beatings that they felt their lives had become terribly insecure. Throughout the South other slave owners made up stories about the Yankees and tried to frighten the slaves. They depicted them as monsters with horns on their heads or warned the slaves that Federal troops were no liberators. They claimed that U.S. soldiers would sell the slaves into a brutal slavery in Cuba or mistreat them horribly.

Such tales had little effect, however, and what whites called the "demoralizing" effects of freedom grew. Some slaves decided that they no longer had to work without pay, so they stopped working or slowed their pace to a level that suited them. As one ex-slave remembered it, "Us slaves worked then when we felt like it, which wasn't offen."[15] Sometimes they gathered for celebrations, possibly killing a pig to roast and enjoy. A South Carolina slaveholder complained that "the Negroes are unwilling to do any work, no matter what it was."[16] Agricultural productivity went down as slave owners' frustration grew.

To get things accomplished, whites began to resort to bargaining—a process that the slaves were adept at, since they always gained something by bringing it into play. As the invading Union army advanced closer to more and more neighborhoods in the South, flight became possible for more slaves. They knew it, and their owners knew it, and that created the context for many bargains. An Alabama owner admitted that he could not exert his authority anymore. He had to beg the slaves to do a little work. In Tennessee, where it became easier for slaves to escape to Union-held Nashville, they pressed their masters for better work routines, even for pay. The slaveholders had to agree or else risk losing their labor force.

Similarly, in eastern North Carolina, where Union forces had occupied the coast, Confederate power waned. One of the largest slave owners in the state, Josiah Collins III, moved with his own family to a safer home and left an overseer to manage the plantation. But controlling Collins's 328 slaves on the insecure coastal plain proved impossible. No longer were the slaves obedient and servile. No longer could the overseer give orders. He told Collins that the slaves spoke about their owner disrespectfully and openly threatened to leave if he made any attempt to control or move them. To avert a mass exodus, the overseer resorted to bribes, admitting that he had to use every possible scheme to keep the slaves on the plantation. He looked the other way when they took plantation goods for their own use, and he even gave hogs and cattle to each family. As for their attitudes toward Josiah Collins, the only polite way to describe their feelings was to say that they did not care for him at all. Slavery's supposedly warm, paternal relations had been a lie. True feelings came to light as the war undermined slavery, and the progress of Northern armies gave slaves more leverage on every plantation, even those more distant from the field of battle.

These realities first puzzled, and then educated, many slaveholders about the reality of the master-slave relationship. Trusted, supposedly "loyal" house slaves ran off to the Yankees, leaving their owners to wonder what had caused this change in their character. Of course, the slaves had simply hidden their true feelings and aspirations. The "faithful slave" in reality was a person who put her faith in freedom, leaving a discouraged and no-longer-deluded owner. As slaves gained confidence that they were to become free, whites declared that they were losing confidence in the black race. Suddenly their servants had become very "unfaithful."

As much as slaves in the Confederacy disappointed unrealistic white Southerners, they proved to be valuable to U.S. soldiers and the Union war effort. In scores of raids and smaller operations that prepared the way for ultimate victory, African Americans readily supplied information and assistance. Their knowledge of the region, with its roads, paths, or waterways, helped Northern soldiers avoid danger and gain military objectives. Captured Union troops found that slaves were their best friends. Alonzo Jackson helped three soldiers escape from a Confederate stockade in Florence, South Carolina. These Yankees were very weak, poorly clothed, and barefoot in the middle of winter. Jackson hid them in his boat and then managed to transport them to U.S. gunboats on the coast. The soldiers were very friendly, grateful, and glad to have such vital help. A white soldier from Maine who also made his escape in South Carolina found that the slaves could not do enough to help him. They brought him and other escapees to their cabins and fed them a nice chicken supper. Then, when it was safe to move, other blacks gave them more food and a guide to take them to safety under the cover of night.

Southern commanders saw the ill effects of the slaves' support for the North. At the end of 1863 one of the Confederacy's best generals, Patrick Cleburne, faced up to a stark reality. The South was on a path to defeat, and slavery was a major part of the problem. In a thoroughly reasoned document signed by several other high-ranking officers, Cleburne pointed out that the South's supply of soldiers was limited. The North, on the other hand, had decided to recruit African Americans into its army, thus subtracting laborers from the South and adding strength to the Union. Moreover, Cleburne argued that slaves were giving ever more valuable information to the enemy. They constituted an unstoppable spy system that operated everywhere. The slaves pointed out Confederate positions, shared news about Confederate plans, and described every locality's resources. Yet they did this so secretly and securely that the Southern army had no way to guard against it. Cleburne, who was one of the few Southerners who could admit that slaves had been dreaming of freedom, declared that slavery had become the Confederacy's greatest vulnerability and a grave source of weakness. The institution that was supposed to be a tower of strength for the South instead became the Confederacy's Achilles' heel.

Nevertheless, for the slaves encounters with Yankee soldiers were not always positive. U.S. troops were sometimes sympathetic, but sometimes hostile. Hardened by war and resentful from suffering their own hardships, they often cared more for themselves than for the slaves they were liberating. Many were strongly racist. Northern black leaders protested to the War Department that some troops were guilty of horrible treatment of the slaves.

The "army . . . seemed more concerned about stealin'," said one bondsman, "than they was about the Holy war for the liberation of the poor African slave people. They took off all de horses, sheeps, cows, chickens, and geese, took the seine and the fishes they caught, corn in crib, meat in smoke-house, everything."[17] Some stole blankets, shoes, or clothing from the slaves, if the army's supplies were inadequate. Slave women were not safe from abuse or rape. Hungry for fresh meat, Yankee troops sometimes slaughtered livestock, and they did it quickly and brutally if they were on the march. "I've seen 'em cut the hams off a live pig or ox and go off leavin' the animal groanin'," said one man.[18] Another slave agreed, calling such mistreatment of animals the meanest thing he had ever seen.

Such actions made life more difficult for the slaves. "All us had to thank them for," said one woman, "was a hungry belly, and freedom."[19] With food on the plantation exhausted, some slaves had to "scour de woods for hickory nuts, acorns, cane roots, and artichokes."[20] The soldiers' destruction brought hunger to more black Southerners than whites, said one slave. Angry over his treatment, one slave berated a soldier for his actions, especially his stealing. "You say you come down here to fight for the [slaves], and now you're stealin' from 'em." In reply this soldier, who was no abolitionist, called the slave a liar and said, "I'm fightin' for $14 a month and the Union."[21]

The temporary presence of Northern troops among white Southerners made it essential for slaves to portray their actions in a way that would most please their owners. Before invading forces arrived, some slaves helped the whites hide horses in the woods or bury silver and valuables in the ground. But they did so under direction and under supervision. Had they revealed these hiding places to the Yankees, they would have had to leave the plantation and follow the troops to be safe. Similarly, when a white woman named Sarah Morgan Dawson had to abandon her town under Federal shelling, she saw slaves carrying their owners' belongings and assumed they did this out of loyalty. Shrewdly, the slaves encouraged her assumption, saying they had not even thought about themselves. Such words pleased the whites and revealed the slaves' awareness of the continuing power relationships that shaped their lives. Martin Jackson remembered his father's insightful advice. He "kept pointing out that the War wasn't going to last forever, but that our forever was going to be spent living among the Southerners, after they got licked."[22]

When U.S. troops tried to help, they sometimes failed to recognize that they were putting the slaves in a difficult position. On one plantation passing Yankee soldiers announced to the slaves that they were free and threw open the smokehouse door. Urging the slaves to enjoy the best of the food, they told them to take all the meat they wanted. At that moment the slaves could have enjoyed a feast. But, recalled one man, "We know they [the soldiers] soon be gone, and then we get a whipping iffen we do."[23] If troops questioned the slaves on their treatment by nearby owners, the slaves had to be very careful in what they said. Lizzie Baker's mother told the troops that her mistress "treat[ed] her right," but she did so only because "ole missus was standin' there, and she was afraid not to say yes."[24]

Still, the prospect of gaining freedom was the answer to years of prayer, the realization of long-deferred dreams. Slaves had longed for freedom. Those held in the Confederacy used the crisis of war to carve out as much liberty as they could, while still enduring bondage. On farms and plantations many were forced to labor for the Confederacy. But many more used the crisis of war to resist their overseers' demands. They slowed production, ignored instructions, and damaged the agricultural goals of the Confederacy. At the same time they gained more living space for themselves and their children. African American slaves proved not to be the tower of strength the Confederacy had predicted, but a debilitating source of weakness. And as black Southerners hurt the Confederate cause, they also advanced the cause of freedom and the Union in both direct and indirect ways.

Indirectly, their day-to-day resistance helped the Union and weakened the Southern army, as it diverted manpower from fighting the North to controlling the home front. Every white Southerner who remained at home to patrol or keep slaves in check was a man who did not fight on the front lines. Every army unit that spent time catching runaways or imposing "order" left that much of a gap in some general's defensive line. Moreover, the determination of slaveholders to guard their human "property" caused conflict with the Confederate government and serious class divisions within Southern society.

The Confederacy was, after all, a government dominated by slaveholders in a society made up primarily of nonslaveholders. Protecting slavery was the motive that inspired secession, and guarding the interests of the slaveholding elite remained central among the goals of legislators. Not surprisingly, various laws and government policies favored slaveholders over nonslaveholders. But as the conditions of life worsened for farmers who owned no slaves, class resentments grew. Why fight for some other man's slaves, poor soldiers began to ask, when neither the government nor prosperous neighbors at home were taking care of a man's wife and children, who went hungry? The suffering of nonslaveholders' families, plus favored treatment for the rich, caused increasing numbers of soldiers to desert and to resist any efforts to send them back to the army.

Slaves directly affected the Confederacy by diminishing production that was crucial to the Southern war effort. From the start Confederate leaders had been overly optimistic about the ability of the slave labor force to keep the agricultural economy running. Under the best of conditions, the South was likely to suffer from a serious shortage of resources. The North was better supplied with men and materials, with essential foodstuffs and industrial products. Then, as the war progressed, the labor and productivity of black Southerners diminished. Sickness and flight reduced the value of the forced labor that the army extorted from impressed slaves. With time slave owners also became more resistant to impressments. Without the great contributions that Confederates had expected from slaves, the South's shortages in resources quickly became more evident and more debilitating.

The Confederacy's slaves also had found many ways to give direct help to the Union armies. Those who could not escape from the South proved to be silent, sure, and effective allies for Union troops. Acting as spies, informants, and secret allies, they assisted invading Federal forces and aided Northern soldiers who were wounded or who had escaped from Southern prisons. The Union benefited greatly from this "omnipresent spy system."

Many others who fled from slavery became part of the Northern war effort. By escaping into Union lines, close to five hundred thousand slaves subtracted their coerced labor from the South and added their active support to the North. Some of those who escaped bondage worked the land and produced goods useful to the North. Others provided a variety of useful services in U.S. army camps.

Thus, slaves in the Confederacy also helped to move the nation toward freedom. Their lives were more difficult than those of free blacks in the North. The great majority of slaves could not taste freedom until the war was over. Many were forced to work for the South. But with quiet determination and shrewd insight into wartime social realities, they interfered with the slaveholders' goal. Their actions damaged the Confederate cause and aided the progress of Union armies—and freedom.

Notes

1. Quoted in James M. McPherson, *The Negro's Civil War* (New York: Ballantine Books, 1965, 1982, 1991), 56.

2. Quoted in Paul D. Escott, *Slavery Remembered* (Chapel Hill: University of North Carolina Press, 1978), 112.

3. Ibid., 76.

4. Ibid.

5. Quoted in David Williams, *I Freed Myself* (New York: Cambridge University Press, 2014), 18.

6. Quoted in Escott, *Slavery Remembered*, 80.

7. Quoted in McPherson, *The Negro's Civil War*, 57.

8. Quoted in Escott, *Slavery Remembered*, 80.

9. Quoted in Ira Berlin, Barbara J. Fields, Steven F. Miller, Joseph P. Reidy, and Leslie Rowland, eds., *Free at Last: A Documentary History of Slavery, Freedom, and the Civil War* (New York: New Press, 1992), 359–60.

10. Ibid., 400–1.

11. Ibid., 107–9.

12. Quoted in Escott, *Slavery Remembered*, 127.

13. Quoted in McPherson, *The Negro's Civil War*, 63.
14. Quoted in Escott, *Slavery Remembered*, 28.
15. Ibid., 122.
16. Quoted in Williams, *I Freed Myself*, 87.
17. Quoted in Escott, *Slavery Remembered*, 123–24.
18. Ibid., 123–24.
19. Ibid., 124.
20. Ibid.
21. Ibid., 124.
22. Ibid., 129.
23. Ibid., 127.
24. Ibid., 127.

CHAPTER THREE

~

Fighting for Freedom, Equality, and the Union

Late in 1862 the U.S. government began to accept African Americans into the armed forces. That was a momentous step. Despite the many problems and injustices that remained, it signaled an important kind of inclusion. In the most severe crisis of the nation, African Americans now shared in its defense. Service in the armed forces implied that black people no longer were aliens who meant nothing to the Union. Instead, they would have a vital role to play. This new era in the government's treatment of blacks caused the editor of the *Pacific Appeal* to hope that "our countrymen are repenting of the great sin they have committed against us for centuries."[1] Philadelphia's Robert Purvis now felt "recognized" as a "citizen of the United States" and rejoiced that change was occurring. "The good time which has so long been coming is at hand. . . . I see it in the new spirit that is in the army. I see it in the black regiment[s]" that are forming.[2]

In both North and South much did begin to change for African Americans. Free black Northerners volunteered and answered the calls for recruitment. In the South increasing numbers of slaves gained their freedom as the Union armies advanced. Once inside Union lines, tens of thousands of these former slaves mustered into the Northern army or put on a navy uniform. Military service was a chance for African American men to prove their manhood, their courage, and their right to a respected place in society. For their wives, children, and elderly relatives who stayed behind, working the land or struggling under difficult conditions to get by, the new era was an opportunity to prove that black people could take advantage of freedom, support themselves, and contribute to the Union.

But much also remained the same. Military necessity had not erased racist attitudes. Black troops faced hostility from many white soldiers and discriminatory policies from the army itself. In Northern cities violence erupted against black residents. Even black war heroes were thrown off streetcars or subjected to discrimination in public places. Southern freed people lived amid insecurity, danger, disease, and neglect. With every gain that African Americans made, there was a racist backlash that tried to deny and reverse their progress. Some whites even scorned the sacrifice of black life on the battlefield.

Still, African American soldiers fought with courage and valor, making an important contribution despite many obstacles. Black leaders used the soldiers' bravery to press their arguments for fair and equal treatment, and they made undeniable progress. With progress and military glory, however, came tragedy and suffering. Heavy losses in combat, massacres at the hands of enraged Confederates, and sickness and death in army or contraband camps were all too common. They were a heavy price to pay, even for freedom and the opportunity to stake a solid claim for citizenship and equal rights.

Facing a severe rebellion, the Northern Congress turned to black soldiers for help. The Second Confiscation Act of July 1862 gave the Federal government legal authority to use black men in the armed forces, but again Congress was ahead of the president. Lincoln worried aloud that arming black men could turn fifty thousand soldiers from the border states against him. Later, in September 1862, he seemed to dismiss the idea of a military role for African Americans. This time he questioned the courage of black men, voicing a fear that if he used black soldiers, in a few weeks their guns would be in the hands of the rebels. The lawmakers and—more importantly—some generals and the secretary of war did not share Lincoln's doubts.

Before the end of 1862 commanders in Louisiana and South Carolina and a U.S. senator in Kansas were beginning to raise black regiments. The War Department approved their actions. At this point, exactly what the role of black soldiers would be remained unclear. When Lincoln issued his final Emancipation Proclamation in January 1863, he spoke of using African Americans to garrison forts or serve on ships. His words seemed to envision a support role, useful but of secondary importance. If black soldiers held on to forts and defended positions already captured, white men could carry the attack deeper into the South.

But as Frederick Douglass and others had argued, the logic of military necessity was driving decisions. That logic became more insistent when the

North resorted to a draft in March of 1863. The army needed more men, and many whites argued that their race should not make all the sacrifices. Lincoln then agreed that black troops would be a splendid asset, and by spring he also concluded that it was time for their families in Union-held territory in the South to prove that they could support themselves by growing their own food.

One of the first Northern states to act was Massachusetts, in January 1863. Governor John Andrew took steps to recruit a black unit, the 54th Massachusetts Regiment, from all parts of the North. He called on white abolitionists like George Stearns and other prominent citizens to raise money for recruitment, and Stearns hired several black leaders as recruiting agents. Among them were the abolitionist minister Henry Highland Garnet, the Ohio attorney and abolitionist John Mercer Langston, and Frederick Douglass. Martin Delany, an abolitionist and former black nationalist, the novelist and well-known lecturer William Wells Brown, and others joined them and began to travel widely, seeking enlistments. Federal policy handicapped their efforts because African Americans could not serve as officers. That policy said, in effect, that blacks were inferior and unfit for leadership. Even worse, the Confederacy was threatening to turn any captured black soldiers over to the Southern states, where they would be sold into slavery or executed as insurrectionists. Some black men also needed encouragement because the war had opened up many new jobs to them they had previously not had access to.

But black leaders and recruiters pressed their arguments to enlist. This was a chance to "show the world by our bravery what the negro can do," said Henry McNeal Turner, who also stressed the moral duty to remember those suffering enslavement in the South.[3] The *Anglo-African* newspaper argued that the impossibility of becoming an officer was trivial compared to having a "chance to settle accounts with the slaveholders."[4] Its editor, Robert Hamilton, predicted that a hundred years might go by before black people would have an equally good opportunity to claim their rights. Frederick Douglass regretted the policy against black officers, but he urged men to join the army and to enlist with the determination to end all forms of racial discrimination. Two of Douglass's own sons soon answered the call. As these arguments took effect, a meeting of blacks in New York City resolved that joining the fight was the appropriate way to support the government, since it was showing greater willingness to respect black people and defend their status. By spring Governor Andrew had enough recruits to launch a second African American regiment, the 55th Massachusetts.

In Washington, D.C., many responded quickly to the new Federal interest in black soldiers. Free black men and contrabands from Virginia declared that their goal was to arrive in Richmond as conquerors. Fighting, they also believed, would do more than support the Union and the Federal government. It was the way to advance black rights. "When we show that we are men," said one advocate of enlistment, "we can then demand our liberty, as did the revolutionary [war] fathers—peaceably if we can, forcibly if we must." If hundreds of thousands of African Americans answered the call to arms, "Would the nation refuse us our rights in such a condition? Would it refuse us our vote? Would it deny us any thing when its salvation was hanging upon us? No! never!"[5]

Recruitment went forward in the North, and more states soon joined the effort in order to satisfy their quotas of troops. Most significant for the raising of troops, however, was Secretary of War Stanton's decision in March to send Adjutant General Lorenzo Thomas into the South to begin recruitment among the escaped slaves. The choice of Lorenzo Thomas seemed a strange one. He and Stanton were not on good terms, and the *Chicago Tribune* noted that Thomas was born in a slave state and had been against black enlistments. But Adjutant General Thomas was a soldier who knew how to take orders. When he arrived in the Mississippi Valley, he immediately went to work and directly confronted the racism among U.S. troops. After learning that escaped slaves has been mistreated by most officers and soldiers, he ordered all troops to treat those who came into Union lines with kindness. Calling white troops together in a series of large meetings, he bluntly told them that the government had a new policy, and it was their duty to obey it. They were to welcome escaped slaves into camp and recruit the men into the service. He threatened to dismiss from the army anyone who mistreated the freedmen, regardless of his rank. By the end of the year twenty-seven thousand black troops were serving in the Mississippi Valley, where Thomas's efforts bore the most fruit.

Some white soldiers loudly objected to serving in an army that included blacks, because white men, they insisted, were racially superior. But as black men came to the Union's aid, their recruitment became an accepted fact. A Northern journalist observed that the loudest opposition to black enlistments was diminishing as the policy produced results. Meanwhile, the War Department took some important steps in May 1863. It established the Bureau of Colored Troops. This bureau took over the organization of black units and regiments, and thereafter it gave the title United States Colored Troops to the many new units. Secretary of War Edwin Stanton also appointed three prominent white Northerners to a newly created American Freedmen's Inquiry Commission, which issued an important report in 1864 on the future status of black Americans.

Recruitment in the loyal border slave states was especially controversial and difficult. These areas were not "in rebellion," so slavery remained legal there. But if recruiters could show that a slave belonged to a Confederate sympathizer, they could ignore the owner's legal claim. Alternatively, slaves could gain their freedom by running away to another state or escaping into a Union army camp, where Federal law encouraged their use in the military. Whites in Missouri, Maryland, and Kentucky tried to hold on to their slaves, but African Americans exploited the situation to gain their freedom. As escapes became ever more numerous, opponents of slavery gained ground in Missouri and Maryland, though Kentucky remained adamantly proslavery. Missouri passed a gradual emancipation ordinance, but that did nothing to stop slaves from leaving their plantations. By July 1863 many army officers in Missouri were ignoring the claims of loyal slaveholders, and recruitment also increased in Maryland. Eventually Lorenzo Thomas established eight recruitment centers in Kentucky as well, where the desire for freedom prevailed over many slaveholders' greed. Before the war ended, nearly 60 percent of black men in Kentucky had joined the Union army—a higher rate than in any slave state.

By the fall of 1864 more than 100,000 black troops were in the field. Before the war ended, almost 180,000 African Americans had served in the army. These enlistments outnumbered all Union fatalities from mid-1863 to the end of the war and thus were a vital contribution to keeping the army strong. Of the total number of black troops, almost 60 percent came from the Confederate states (where most blacks were), and almost a quarter from the border states that remained in the Union. The free black men who enrolled in the North were a smaller percentage of all African American troops, but their numbers represented a very high rate of enlistment.

Slaves who escaped into Union lines from the Confederacy often were eager to join the army. They wanted to play a role in destroying slavery and defeating the slaveholders' new nation. A white officer who interviewed his recruits bluntly reminded one man that he might lose his life in military service. "But my people will be free," responded this former slave.[6] Others like him were eager to strike a blow against the institution that had caused their suffering.

There were other motives for enlistment. Black women often encouraged their husbands or sons to join the army and help liberate their race. As one woman pushed her husband toward the ranks of volunteers, she told him that he was more attractive standing among the brave men who were enlisting. It also was the case that army officers frequently used threats to force men to join the army or work for it. In many Union camps, officers told escaped

Thousands of escaped slaves who did not fight did heavy labor for the U.S. army, like these men in Virginia. Often their food, clothing, and shelter were inadequate. Courtesy Library of Congress, Prints and Photographs Division, Gladstone Collection of African American Photographs.

slaves that the women and children could have food and shelter there only if the men agreed to put on a uniform.

Donning that uniform did not always mean that black troops were allowed to play the role they desired. Instead of fighting, many African American soldiers found that they were relegated to support roles and heavy labor. Although men on guard duty put Bibles and spelling books under their belts and studied reading when not on duty, this was not the soldiering they desired. White racism caused many officers to doubt that blacks could be good warriors. General William Tecumseh Sherman was the most prominent example of this attitude, and Sherman's prestige allowed him to avoid using blacks in combat roles. Whites generally assumed that former slaves were better suited than Northern whites to labor under the hot southern sun. Consequently, many officers ordered black soldiers to labor—building forts, digging trenches, or unloading ships and wagons. They also were given the least desirable jobs, such as cleaning latrines, only to find that prejudiced whites looked down on them for doing the dirty work.

This pattern was most common in the western armies, where blacks frequently served as the army of occupation that allowed white soldiers to fight elsewhere. A member of the Massachusetts 54th protested that "we are not

Soldiers but Laborers working for Uncle Sam for nothing but our board and clothes . . . it is nothing but work from morning till night Building Batteries Hauling Guns Cleaning Bricks . . . now do you call this Equality if so, God help such Equality."[7] General Lorenzo Thomas, to his credit, tried to end this practice. He issued an order in June 1864 that instructed his commanders to be fair and impartial in the assignment of fatigue duty. Thomas could not supervise every officer, however, and a man with the standing of General Sherman was beyond Thomas's control. Sherman refused to believe that blacks could be good warriors. He was willing to use them only in menial roles. If Sherman let black troops staff a local garrison, he felt he was taking enough risk with an inferior race.

Inequality was the rule even in the fundamental matter of pay. The Militia Act passed in 1862 had set the pay of white privates at $13 per month, with $3.50 added each month as a clothing allowance. In the expectation that African Americans would serve mainly as laborers, that law set their wages at $10 per month, from which $3 was deducted for the expense of clothing. To make matters worse, often this meager pay was late or long delayed in coming. Black troops protested against these inequities, both as a matter of principle and for practical reasons. Black soldier Thomas Sipple worried that his family would be suffering back home because they needed his pay. Not knowing when he could help his loved ones, Sipple complained that the army was treating him and his comrades like rebels. Corporal James Henry Gooding, a highly intelligent and educated man from Massachusetts, wrote directly to President Lincoln. "Are we Soldiers, or are we Labourers?" he asked. African American soldiers "have dyed the ground with blood, in defense of the Union. . . . Now your Excellency, we have done a Soldier's Duty. Why Can't we have a Soldier's pay?"[8]

Black leaders in the North joined these protests and worked for fair treatment for the soldiers. Frederick Douglass managed to raise the issue with Abraham Lincoln, who told him that voters still had grave objections to making black men soldiers. Since their enlistment seriously offended white prejudice, Lincoln viewed lower pay as a necessary concession if the army wanted to use blacks as soldiers at all. Lincoln said a remedy for the situation would come eventually, but black leaders continued to protest. The editor of the *Christian Recorder* protested on behalf of all the men who were risking their lives for the Union cause, only to be mistreated. He called on Congress to pass a law, immediately, providing for equal pay. Reverend J. P. Campbell of the AME Church warned that discrimination in pay would damage recruitment. Black soldiers had a right to expect equal pay, he insisted, and their service in war should lead to equal rights and privileges once combat was over.

The matter of equal rights was fundamental to black leaders. J. W. C. Pennington reminded whites that black people had helped the nation gain independence from Britain. Now the nation was at war to overcome Jefferson Davis and his fellow secessionists, and black people were in the fight. Black soldiers risked their lives, he declared, with the understanding that they were entitled to gain all their rights. To Frederick Douglass the goal was admission "as a full member in good and regular standing in the American body politic." The African American soldier who "bare[s] his breast to the storm of rebel artillery . . . knows enough to vote." Any restrictions on voting, "whether of intelligence or wealth," must apply equally to all races, insisted Douglass.[9] An important meeting of Northern black leaders declared that military service and sacrifice proved the manhood of African Americans and demanded respect from the civilized world.

Ex-slaves from the South believed just as strongly in the necessity of equal rights. Abraham Galloway was a former slave from coastal North Carolina who repeatedly showed great courage and dedication to freedom. On many occasions he slipped into Confederate territory and returned days or weeks later, leading dozens of slaves to freedom in Union-held areas along the coast. With four other black men from his state, he called on President Lincoln in the spring of 1864. "All men are created equal," they reminded the president (who revered the Declaration of Independence), and they asked him "to finish the noble work you have begun" by securing the right to vote for black Americans. "We have contributed moral and physical aid to our country in her hour of need, and expect to do so until every cloud of war shall disappear."[10] In return African Americans should gain their rights.

Meanwhile African American troops encountered frequent mistreatment in establishing their claim to equality. They faced hostility from Northern soldiers and greater danger if captured by the Southern rebels. Racial slurs were common, as many Union troops believed they were superior. Even many white officers leading black regiments assumed that blacks had little intelligence and were physically and mentally inferior. Although some of these white officers had volunteered out of idealism, others simply wanted to gain a promotion or better pay. A few defrauded their troops, confiscated savings that had been entrusted to them, or stole the soldiers' pay. The *Anglo-African* reported numerous instances of horrible treatment of blacks by white U.S. troops.

Mistreatment from Confederates posed another danger. The Union's white soldiers knew they would be prisoners of war if captured. But the Confederacy refused to consider black men wearing the Union uniform as soldiers. Instead, it regarded them as criminals and threatened to execute or send into slavery any black troops it captured. At first Abraham Lincoln issued a stern statement in protest. He announced that the United States would execute one rebel soldier for every black man killed in violation of the laws of war. For any Union troops enslaved, he said that his government would put an equal number of rebel soldiers at hard labor. Unfortunately, Lincoln did not enforce his policy. In the end he shrank from retaliation against Confederate prisoners. He told Frederick Douglass that he was not enforcing his warning because he feared that retaliation, once begun, would never end.

How, then, could African Americans counter prejudice within the army and establish their rights in society? It was in battle that they hoped to win respect and change their status.

The test of battle came quickly for black troops. With little training, black soldiers found themselves in fierce combat along the Mississippi River in the summer of 1863. Fighting against overwhelming numbers, or struggling to advance over impossible terrain, they suffered heavy casualties.

Taking control of the Mississippi River was a major objective of the Union army. If the North could seize the river, it would cut the Confederacy in two and thus prevent resources and soldiers in the Trans-Mississippi West from coming to the aid of the eastern parts of the Confederacy. By the spring of 1863 the Union had seized New Orleans and held various points along the northern reaches of the Mississippi River. But Port Hudson, to the north of Baton Rouge, and Vicksburg, about halfway up the river between New Orleans and Memphis, remained as major objectives still left to take. Both were naturally strong defensive positions, made more secure by Confederate fortifications and artillery. Milliken's Bend was a key site in the defenses of Vicksburg.

In May 1863 General Nathaniel Banks began a series of operations to seize Port Hudson. On May 26, two units of the Louisiana Native Guards, composed of free blacks and mixed-race men from the New Orleans area, went into action. Lacking wagons, they had made a hard march with all their baggage in oppressive heat, and then had gone to work building a pontoon bridge over Big Sandy Creek near its junction with the Mississippi River. The next morning, Union forces, including the Louisiana Native Guards, began an attack on the well-defended fort. The soldiers had to advance over swampy ground and rough terrain that was covered with pine trees and magnolias. At 10 a.m., when the Union advance was grinding to a halt, the order came for the 1st and 3rd Louisiana Native Guards to attack. Their assault faced converging enemy fire—from both the fort to their front and from a ridge to their left. To reach the fort's breastworks, men had to wade through water that was chest high, and in some places eight feet deep.

The Louisiana soldiers rushed forward into a hurricane of fire that lasted fifteen minutes. When they had come within two hundred yards of the Confederates' main line, rebel artillery fired canister shot from their cannon, sending hundreds of lead balls toward the troops. The battle flag of the 1st Louisiana Native Guards was torn by so many projectiles that it almost fell off its staff. Three men, acting in series, tried to keep the flag aloft, until each one was killed or wounded. Captain Andre Cailloux, a leader of New Orleans's free Afro-French Creole community, had his left arm shattered above the elbow but continued to lead his men forward. At a point only fifty yards from the Confederate line, he fell, mortally wounded. Other soldiers tried to fight on despite wounds. One man, whose leg had been shot off beneath the knee, managed to fire thirty rounds before being carried to the rear. The bodies of dead Native Guardsmen soon were floating in the Mississippi's backwaters.

The assault, ordered by a drunken colonel, was hopeless. The Louisiana troops had to retreat, along with all the other Union men engaged that day. The Confederate defenses at Port Hudson did not fall until July 9, after a

Black troops saw heavy fighting in 1863. This image of "A Negro Regiment in Action" appeared in *Harper's Weekly*, a very popular magazine. From *Harper's Weekly*, March 14, 1863, courtesy archive.org.

long siege. These first black soldiers to be involved in an intense battle suffered heavy casualties. One military historian estimates that the two Louisiana units, though only 4 percent of the Union troops present, suffered at least 20 percent of all Union casualties that day. More than one-third of their men died, and another 14 percent or 15 percent were wounded.

But as General Banks told his wife in a private letter, undeniably they had fought courageously and well and met every expectation. Such a performance, Banks concluded, removed any doubt that African American troops could be efficient and effective. Other soldiers who had been on the scene agreed. The courage and daring of the black troops banished the doubts of a white lieutenant who had taken part in the fighting. Another man, a captain, praised their superb efforts, which gave the lie to all the popular theories about black deficiencies. A colonel agreed. For him the bravery of the Louisiana Native Guards settled the question of black combat abilities beyond question.

Reports of this first deadly contest involving African Americans had some effect in the North. White newspapers in major cities published accounts of the battle. The *Chicago Tribune* quoted General Banks's assessment of black troops. The *New-York Daily Tribune* judged that they had fought gallantly. Headlines in the *New York Times* publicized the great bravery of the 1st and 3rd Louisiana Native Guards. It also pointed out that they had made six separate charges against the Confederates' position. For the *Times* this proved that blacks could fight with great skill, and the *Cincinnati Gazette* quoted several observers who praised the troops for fighting with the desperation of tigers. The *Gazette*'s local rival, the *Cincinnati Daily Enquirer*, favored the Democratic Party, but in what would prove to be unusually objective reporting for Democratic newspapers, it too credited the outstanding bravery of the black troops. This initial reaction helped Lincoln's Republican administration gain support for black enlistments, and it also stimulated volunteering among free black men in the North. Recruiting posters celebrated Port Hudson and highlighted the courage and heroism of the Louisiana troops.

Little more than a month later, African American soldiers again were involved in a bloody battle, this time at Milliken's Bend, fifteen miles northwest of Vicksburg. General Grant was using the location as a staging area for his siege against the city. The Confederates attacked from the western side of the Mississippi River as part of an effort to lift the siege. The defense of General Grant's supplies and hospitals at Milliken's Bend fell to experienced white and newly enrolled black troops, most of them former slaves. The former slaves had had very little training or drill, and had been organized into regiments only a few weeks previously. Their weapons were of poor quality.

In battle they had to rely far more on native courage than on military training or knowledge of tactics.

What ensued, according to a white officer who was the veteran of much larger battles, was a terrific struggle, worse even than the bloody battle of Shiloh. Union forces formed a defensive line in front of an eight-foot-high levee located about 150 yards from the Mississippi River. To the soldiers' front were a series of thorny hedges, through which the Confederate attackers had to come. There was a large gap in the hedge directly in front of the position taken by the black troops of the 9th Louisiana Regiment. They had no line of retreat, except to swim the river.

Just after dawn the Confederates attacked. Rushing the Union positions, they evaded the Union fire, which was ineffective, and soon reached the levee. For long minutes there was bloody, hand-to-hand combat with troops using their bayonets or swinging their rifle stocks as clubs. Bayonets inflicted only a tiny portion of all the wounds in the Civil War, but here they prevailed. The black troops of the 9th Louisiana followed orders to hold their fire and used their bayonets whenever possible. One powerful black soldier named Jack Johnson attracted attention from both sides. He leapt at the attacking Confederates, smashing heads with the wooden stock of his rifle. Before long he had nothing left of his gun but the barrel, so he continued to swing it at the rebels' heads. Shouting racial epithets, Confederates focused their fire on Jack Johnson and eventually killed him. Then some Texas troops yelled "No quarter," indicating that they wanted to kill every black soldier and take no prisoners.

The Union forces had to fall back to the river, where they were able to find some natural shelter on the riverbank because the water was low. There they kept up a resistance, and soon a Union gunboat, the *Choctaw*, arrived to heave shells at the Confederates. This artillery barrage, plus the arrival of additional gunboats and exhaustion among the rebel forces, who had marched much of the previous night, brought the battle to an end. Federal troops had lost about half of their entire garrison, and the African American soldiers had the greatest losses. More than two-thirds of all the blacks troops engaged had been killed or wounded. There is controversy over whether Confederate soldiers slaughtered black Unionists who could have been taken prisoner. But the rebel commander, General Richard Taylor, admitted as much when he said that, unfortunately, his troops took fifty Union prisoners.

Though the combat at Milliken's Bend had no strategic importance, it did convince some whites that black soldiers deserved respect. The remarkable courage of one black company left its white officer from Illinois sick at heart. All but one of the thirty-three black men in that unit lost their lives or suffered wounds. The African American soldiers were raw recruits, had just received their rifles, and had benefited from little training. Yet they had distinguished themselves in battle and proved their character. White observers now knew that blacks would fight, and fight well. The common remark among wounded white survivors was that the blacks fought like tigers.

Such praise reached the highest levels of the War Department. An assistant secretary of war who had been visiting General Grant reported on events to Secretary of War Stanton. Attitudes in the army about using black troops, he wrote, should undergo a revolution now that the men at Milliken's Bend had demonstrated their bravery. Officers on the scene had replaced their racial sneers with respect for black courage and now were in favor of using more black soldiers. Lorenzo Thomas commented on how rare it was for bayonets to dominate in a Civil War battle. That reality at Milliken's Bend gave irrefutable evidence of the dependability of black troops. Unfortunately on this occasion, many large Northern newspapers, except the *Chicago Tribune*, did not cover the battle. The *Tribune* gave full credit to black soldiers, but in many other cities the battle near Vicksburg was overshadowed by events in Charleston.

In July 1863, the 54th Massachusetts—already an object of notice—made a courageous charge against Fort Wagner in Charleston Harbor. Led by Colonel Robert Gould Shaw, a white abolitionist from a prominent Boston family, the African Americans of the 54th Massachusetts attracted still more attention as they went into battle, and their bravery showed that they merited it. After making two tiring marches, they arrived before the fort at 6 p.m., tired and wet, thirsty and hungry. After a brief rest, the order to attack came. Charging across a narrow stretch of sand, the men of the 54th Massachusetts encountered a murderous fire from the fort's defenders. Large numbers of men were cut down before they came close to the fort, but the survivors never faltered and kept coming. As the *New-York Daily Tribune* reported, they "dashed through the ditches, gained the parapet, and engaged in a hand-to-hand fight with the enemy, and for nearly half-an-hour held their ground, and did not fall back until nearly every commissioned officer was shot down."[11] Colonel Shaw himself was killed, along with men who had vowed to follow him into death and who kept their promise.

Those who survived were lucky, as the grape and canister and rifle shots mowed down most of the attackers like a scythe running through grass. The fact that many men had kept coming and challenged the Confederates in hand-to-hand combat caused military men to praise the black soldiers' great bravery. Such valor attracted considerable praise in Northern newspapers. The *New-York Daily Tribune*, for example, said that they had done everything possible and gave abundant proof of heroism. A white abolitionist, Angelina Grimké Weld, rejoiced somewhat prematurely that newspapers, even a few Democratic papers, were praising black soldiers. One month later General Grant told the president that using black troops had his full support. Grant believed that arming blacks, together with the Emancipation Proclamation, constituted the heaviest blow yet given to the Confederacy. On August 26 Lincoln scolded opponents of emancipation and black troops by writing, in a public letter, that in future years black Americans would be able to remember that they had risked their lives courageously for freedom and the Union, while some white men stood aside and hindered the cause.

Angelina Weld's rejoicing was premature because racism remained deeply rooted and widely shared in American society. With each advance in black rights, there was a racist backlash. The fact that African Americans were gaining ground caused some opponents to fight them more fiercely. In addition, the unwelcome changes and the economic and social stresses brought on by the war irritated racial conflicts and spurred some people to blame their problems on the Negro. At the same time that African Americans were validating their claim to freedom and citizenship, ugly antiblack riots broke out in major cities. Partisan spokesmen and newspapers also refused to credit the black soldiers' accomplishments or twisted the facts to achieve racist ends.

The first major riot of 1863 broke out in Detroit in March, and was based on nothing more than rumor and racial enmity. Stories spread that a black man had raped a white orphan or that he operated a saloon that was a "den" of interracial sex. A mob gathered and started smashing windows, beating against doors, and shouting racist curses. A black man named Joshua Boyd died at the hands of the mob. Many other blacks in Detroit fled the town in fear, testifying that they "wandered all the night in the woods, with nothing to eat, nor covering from the cold." By morning some had "frosted feet" and found to their sorrow that "all our property [was] destroyed."[12] An aggravating factor in the Detroit violence was resentment over the draft. Whites who did not want to be drafted blamed the war on African Americans. They shouted that they would kill all the black people whose presence in America had dragged white people into the war.

Opposition to the draft lit the fuse of a much bigger riot in New York City. Many recently arrived immigrants, often from Ireland, were resistant to being called into the war. They also suspected that the draft lists were unfair, with poor neighborhoods having to furnish the bulk of the men while rich men could pay a "commutation" of $300 and stay out of the army. These immigrants generally were in competition with blacks for the lower-paying jobs that were available. On Monday, July 13, 1863, a protest against the draft quickly turned violent. Demonstrators that had begun the day carrying signs demanding "No Draft" by the afternoon were venting their rage on any black person they could find.

Rioters shouted murderous threats against black people and against Republicans for showing any concern for blacks. The mob beat up a nine-year-old boy, and then four hundred rioters descended on the Colored Orphan Asylum. "Burn the niggers' nest," they shouted. The staff was able to evacuate all but one little girl, who was killed, and then the mob stole or broke up and burned all the asylum's furniture. Later that day a black man was hanged, and the violence sparked three more days of terrifying mob actions.

On the second day, violence focused even more on local black residents; the riot became a hunt for African Americans. A black man named William Jones went out to buy a loaf of bread for breakfast, but the mob caught him, hung him from a tree, and lit a fire beneath him. As Jones died, the rioters pelted his body with stones. Other blacks were stripped of their clothes, beaten, kicked and stomped on, knifed, drowned, or hanged. Elderly men, as old as seventy years of age, and young children, who were too young to understand what was going on, met their deaths. The bodies of some victims were mutilated, and a report by a committee of New York merchants later said that there had been atrocities too indecent to describe in any publication.

New York City's police were ineffective or overwhelmed, and the U.S. military had to intervene to stop the violence. Five regiments of soldiers who had just been at Gettysburg were ordered to the city to restore order. It was one of the worst riots in the nation's history, and what had begun as a protest against the draft ended as an attack on the entire black community. Before the riots were over, thousands of black people had lost their property, suffered wounds, or endured terror. An accurate count of the dead was impossible, but historians believe that at least 105 died. The riot's destruction left five thousand people homeless, and nearly three thousand received relief that the merchants later organized. The popular magazine *Harper's Weekly* commented on the painful irony of events. "It was at the very hour when negroes were pouring out their blood for the stars and stripes on the slopes of Fort Wagner that naturalized foreigners, who hauled down the Stars and Stripes whenever they saw them, tried to exterminate the negro race in New York."[13]

Political partisanship fed societal racism and made progress for African Americans more difficult. The Democratic Party scorned black abilities, defended Southern rights, and denounced emancipation. Its newspapers had charged that Lincoln was destroying the Constitution. Now they waged a propaganda campaign against black troops, ignoring the courage of black soldiers, flatly denying their contributions, and inventing alternate versions of reality to support racism. After Port Hudson and Milliken's Bend, one black Philadelphian complained that "the infernal Copper-heads are incensed and will not publish the true statements."[14] For example, one Democratic paper claimed in the weeks after the fighting at Port Hudson that attempts to train black troops were a total failure and always would be, since the freed slaves were lazy and useless. To a Cincinnati newspaper the use of black soldiers disgraced the government and would bring shame to Americans because the black race supposedly was barbaric. Other white newspapers repeated old lies about black people being lazy and incompetent. When Republican papers praised black troops, Democratic editors branded that praise as an insult to white soldiers, claiming that their valor was being ignored. According to the Democrats, the aim of Lincoln's administration was to make the black man better than the white man and force intermarriage on a superior white race. One Democratic journal claimed that black officers enjoyed superior rank over white officers, despite the fact that almost no African Americans served as officers during the Civil War.

The status of the black soldier remained a sore point with anyone who cared about justice until the last days of the war. Abolitionists and friends in Congress fought to end the discrimination in pay and give black troops a chance to be officers. They arranged for Congress to hear testimony from military commanders who praised the bravery, enthusiasm, and coolness under fire of black soldiers. When the government called for more men, black veterans petitioned to raise "colored regiments, to be officered exclusively by colored men."[15] A meeting of African Americans in Philadelphia resolved that there was no good reason why African Americans should not be promoted to command colored troops. The refusal to commission black officers was unjust and an "insulting endorsement of the old dogma of negro inferiority."[16] Yet on this point they failed almost completely. Most black soldiers who eventually held an officer's rank were chaplains or surgeons, rather than lieutenants or captains who commanded in the field. The few officers' commissions that the War Department granted came late, in the closing days of the war.

The struggle for equal pay turned out only slightly better and, on balance, left a record more discouraging than encouraging. In December 1863, Secretary of War Edwin Stanton urged Congress to equalize the pay of black and white soldiers, and he had support from abolitionist congressmen and senators, such as Thaddeus Stevens and Charles Sumner. Black soldiers demanded to know "Why are we not worth as much as white soldiers? We do the same work they do. . . . We fight as well as they do."[17] Reverend J. P. Campbell of the AME Church emphasized in Baltimore that African Americans were protesting over the principle of equal pay and equal rights, not money. Black leaders like William Wells Brown and John Rock resigned as recruiters in protest over the pay issue, and Rock declared that black soldiers had "covered themselves all over with glory" and deserved the same treatment that whites expected and received.[18] The *Christian Recorder* editorialized that it was receiving angry letters from black troops and warned of demoralization in the ranks. White commanders agreed that the failure to correct this injustice might demoralize the troops.

Black troops were angry not only about the inequality in pay but also about the frequent *absence* of pay. The army was scandalously inefficient, even irresponsible, in paying its troops, and especially its black units. Often pay arrived late, sometimes very late, and after a year had gone by the proper description seemed to be never at all. Without pay the families of black soldiers, especially from the urban North, suffered greatly. One soldier wrote that after six months without receiving a penny, his wife and three small children had neither adequate food nor fuel in the winter. There was a near mutiny in the 55th Massachusetts in 1864, and both the 54th and 55th Massachusetts regiments refused to accept any pay—even from the state, which tried to help—until the injustice was removed.

But white racism stalled and delayed action in Congress. The tragic fact was that many white Americans did not want to see blacks advance. The Democratic *New York World*, for example, insisted that using black soldiers degraded the status of white men and was unjust to the superior race. Finally, in June 1864 Congress passed a law giving equal pay that was retroactive to January 1, 1864, for all black troops and retroactive to the time of enlistment for those individuals who had been free at the beginning of the war. That wording failed to give full justice to the many escaped slaves who had served in 1863. Moreover, the different retroactive provisions created a morale problem among men who had fought in battle side by side. An officer of the 54th Massachusetts cleverly decided to let the men who had escaped from slavery swear that they had not owed labor to Southern masters when the war began. Other units followed that example, and there was a great celebration in the 55th Massachusetts's camp. Its men rejoiced because they had been waiting for eighteen months for both pay and fair treatment.

In a sense the matter of pay was emblematic of the overall experience of black soldiers. They gave much, they suffered much, and they gained much, though they never received all that they deserved. The war record of African

Americans—as soldiers, contrabands, and noncombatants—was an impressive one. They helped make enormous progress against profound injustices in American society. But their experience was also a heartbreakingly sad and tragic one, as the price they paid was high, both on the battlefield and in Union-held portions of the South. To the suffering caused by bullets, unfair policies, and prejudice has to be added the pain encountered due to insecurity, disease, and death.

African Americans made a major military contribution, despite the government's refusal to let them serve until very late in 1862. Overall, they took part in forty-one major battles and 449 minor skirmishes. They fought and died in some of the most important battles of the war, including the Battle of Nashville, which decimated the army of Confederate General John Bell Hood, and the Battle of Petersburg, which came before Lee's surrender at Appomattox. During the final Union invasion of Virginia in 1864 and 1865, fifteen black regiments served in the Army of the James and twenty-three in the Army of the Potomac. African Americans took part in all the other major campaigns of 1864–1865 except for Sherman's march through Georgia. As infantry, artillery, and even cavalry, they won praise from several white generals. After the Battle of Nashville, for example, the Union commander, General George Thomas, declared that they had proved their fighting ability beyond any question. The Congressional Medal of Honor went to seventeen black soldiers and four black sailors.

Still, most African American troops served behind the lines, garrisoning forts in the Mississippi Valley and guarding supply lines. That meant that they participated in fewer major battles than whites and overall suffered fewer casualties. But they took advantage of every opportunity to fight and almost always fought with great determination. The highly respected historian Joseph Glatthaar has noted that black units often suffered casualties at a higher rate than white units. The reason was that they took greater risks to perform well, and lost many more lives, because they wanted to prove their courage and value. Black troops knew that they were fighting not only for the Union but also for progress for their race.

At least forty thousand, and perhaps a third, of all black troops were reported as killed in action, died of wounds or disease, or missing. As was the case with white troops, a large portion of the deaths came as the result of disease. The Civil War occurred before the advent of lifesaving drugs or even an understanding of the role of bacteria in causing illness. Due to flawed ideas of sanitation, polluted water, and the crowding together of men from different regions and disease environments, sickness took a heavy toll. More than twenty-nine thousand black men died from dysentery, typhoid fever, pneumonia, and malaria. Fatigue labor, deficient housing, poor rations, and duty in low-lying and malarial regions along the Mississippi increased the danger for many.

Sadly, poor medical care by the army was a significant part of the problem for black soldiers. Although the death rate from disease was one in seventeen for white soldiers, it was a shocking one in seven for black troops. Part of the reason was discriminatory medical care. A surgeon in a black regiment admitted that very few of the army's doctors gave the same care to blacks as to whites. General Lorenzo Thomas was horrified when he inspected a hospital for United States Colored Troops in Nashville. In lice-infested wards he found men still wearing the blood-soaked uniforms in which they had arrived from the battlefield. Appalled and sickened by what he saw, Thomas angrily noted that white soldiers never would have experienced such neglect.

Discrimination left its mark on the battlefield as well, where Confederates retaliated against men who wanted to be free and Northern whites acted with prejudice. The most notable massacre of black Union soldiers by Confederates took place at the battle of Fort Pillow, a Union position on the Mississippi River north of Memphis. In April 1864 rebel forces under General Nathan Bedford Forrest attacked the fort. With more than twice as many men as Fort Pillow's 570 defenders, Forrest was able to drive the Union forces into the garrison's innermost defenses. After the Union commander refused to surrender, Confederates stormed the fort and gained control.

One black soldier, Duncan Hardin Winslow, was lucky to escape with his life. Winslow remembered Confederate soldiers screaming "Kill the God damned nigger" as soon as they saw him.[19] Then, after Union soldiers repeatedly tried to surrender, the killing continued, with blacks as a special target. "Damn you, you are fighting against your master," cried one Southerner, who then shot Private George Shaw in the face. Black U.S. Private Eli Carlton later testified, "I saw 23 men shot after they surrendered; I made 24."[20] A few Confederate officers tried to stop the slaughter, but some Confederate privates declared that they would not take a black soldier prisoner. Most of the victims from the battle at Fort Pillow were African Americans. The massacre there became widely known, but it was only one of a number of similar wartime atrocities against United States Colored Troops.

Northern prejudices played a role in the sadly disappointing outcome of the Battle of the Crater, which occurred during the Union siege of Petersburg, Virginia, in 1864. Experienced coal miners in the Union army had secretly and successfully dug a long tunnel that extended beneath the Confederate army's defenses. At the end of this tunnel they placed a massive charge of explosives. The plan was to detonate that subterranean bomb, blow a large hole in the enemy's line, and then attack through that gap, routing the Southern army and opening the route to Richmond. It was an innovative and promising idea.

Originally, black units were going to have the honor and the opportunity of spearheading the attack, right after the bomb went off. One brigade would advance to the left of the crater, and the other would break through by going to the right of the crater. But Union commanders still had doubts about the courage and ability of black troops, and at the last minute they changed the orders and sent white units into action first. These white troops, unprepared, poorly instructed, and without good leadership, made the mistake of rushing *into* the crater, where they quickly became mired in the soft earth. By the time black troops were ordered to follow them, the Confederates had recovered from their surprise and were massed in defense at the crater's sides. Black and white Union soldiers made good targets, as the rebels enjoyed a murderous form of target practice. Although many black soldiers tried to surrender, the Confederates murdered them on the spot. General Grant felt that this botched attack was the saddest operation he had seen in the entire war.

But it was not just the black soldiers who suffered greatly and died in disproportionate numbers. Throughout the occupied portions of the South, black women, children, and older adults who were left behind when their husbands, sons, and brothers joined the army did their part to aid the Union but paid a heavy price as well. Deprived of their strongest male labor force, what these people were able to accomplish was impressive. But what they suffered—due to the conditions and tides of war but even more due to the Union's unpreparedness, neglect, and lack of concern—was appalling.

From the beginning the Federal government was improvising as it decided what to do with the slaves who came under Union control. The "contrabands" who freed themselves by escaping into Union lines, and the slaves who lived in areas that the Union conquered, were equally a challenge and a problem for the army. The escaped slaves needed some kind of shelter, food, and protection in a war zone. Too often they never received vital support because the army always hoped this could be done without too much complication or expense. In the Union's contraband camps, army tents provided shelter, but commanders pressured African Americans to aid the army and find ways of supporting themselves. They also appointed special agents from the military to organize, supervise, and aid the freedmen.

As Federal forces conquered portions of the fertile Mississippi Valley, new arrangements arose. In some places the military itself supervised abandoned plantations or allowed planters who swore loyalty to continue running their plantations, but under a new regime, supposedly, of freedom. In other places commanders leased plantations to Northern businessmen, who sought to make them productive for themselves and the government. Both the War Department and the Treasury Department, at times, were involved in these arrangements.

Whatever the system, Northerners were keenly interested in the attitudes, behavior, and accomplishments of the African Americans who had moved out of the world of slavery. How would they act? Would they work, asked many prejudiced whites? Were they too ignorant, lazy, or degraded to care for themselves? Would they be a permanent burden on the government, as many Democratic newspapers claimed? In short, prejudiced Northerners wondered if there was a place in America's competitive, free-labor society for former slaves.

The black women, children, and older adults who did not enlist in the army faced many disadvantages. Usually they had migrated to a new place and had left homes, tools, and clothing behind to strike out in a new environment. They were without the most productive part of an agricultural labor force—the adult men who had gone into the army. It would not be easy for them to banish the doubts and prejudices of whites, but from an early date they started to do so. Even women who had no land to farm or no employment in the contraband camps found ways to support themselves as laundresses, cooks, or servants to army officers. Soon they were proving that free labor was workable.

In the Sea Islands, the freedmen on abandoned plantations quickly proved themselves. The blacks on the islands were working steadily and with a will, despite the racist stereotype of lazy slaves. The freedmen were industrious, especially when there were decent wages or the prospect of a reward for their labor. At the same time, blacks wanted to have their own land, and they objected when the government failed to pay for work done. Army officers who were in charge of freedmen at other points along the southeastern coast agreed. The former slaves were ready to work, and work well, as long as they could expect to receive a reasonable wage. A supervisor in the Department of the South wrote that he never had seen an instance in which a former slave declined to work, as long as he had the chance to earn even moderate wages. Businessmen and investors who came to these occupied territories reached the same conclusion. By 1864 Rufus Saxton, the military governor of blacks in the Sea Island region, reported that the former slaves had demonstrated that they could advance under a system of free labor.

Elsewhere, in the Upper South or on Union-held farms in Virginia, blacks showed the same readiness to work that impressed army officers. The superintendent of contrabands in Virginia admitted that he was surprised and revised his opinion that black people lacked intelligence. In intelligence they proved themselves equal to the whites, and 78 percent of the blacks under his supervision had become independent of any government assistance. In Union-held areas of Louisiana the results also were good wherever plantations were well and fairly managed. But the former slaves resisted working for their old overseers, who retained the routines and controls of slavery. Along with their willingness to work, the former slaves had a new spirit of independence, and they refused to work for the old slaveholders. Their goal was to cultivate land of their own.

Even before the end of 1862, the *New-York Daily Tribune* drew on army reports to show that the freedmen demonstrated a firm loyalty to the Federal government and no signs of laziness or unreliability. In addition to working hard and well, the freedmen showed that they were hungry to obtain an education, which was an important way to advance themselves. By the beginning of 1865 hundreds of thousands of ex-slaves were farming under Union supervision or for the Union's benefit, especially in the Mississippi Valley. The results of these arrangements had proved that men and women who had been scorned as slaves were fully capable of earning their own living. Not only had they fed themselves and grown valuable crops helpful to the Union, but they also had made money to buy tools and work animals. In the unsettled and shifting conditions of war, it was remarkable that they had accomplished so much in this experiment of free black labor.

The difficulties of this experiment were, in fact, formidable. In Louisiana the Union authorities themselves had made many counterproductive decisions. Initially General Nathaniel Banks established rules for work on plantations that were all too reminiscent of slavery days. When planters took the loyalty oath, Banks required that black workers show respectful behavior and act with the kind of subordination that slaveholders had always expected. Any "insolence" would cause a loss of wages, and Banks indicated that the government would enforce these expectations. Black Louisianans objected, and some moderate and Radical Republicans in Congress complained that what Banks had created was a "serf system." Frederick Douglass declared that it "practically enslaves the negro" and turns the Emancipation Proclamation into "a mockery and delusion."[21] Even in 1864 things were not markedly better. A member of the American Freedmen's Inquiry Commission judged the authorized wages to be shamefully low, and it was inexcusable that on many plantations whipping was still permitted. In other parts of the South, as well, there were supervisors or lessees who treated the freedmen unfairly, selfishly, or deceitfully.

But the causes of an enormous amount of suffering, and many thousands of deaths, were more basic and were inherent in the wartime situation and white indifference. What had been a small Federal government suddenly was fighting a massive war. Bureaucratic inadequacies and inefficiencies were probably to be expected and proved to be all too common. Battle lines and military needs changed from week to week or month to month. Commanders who understood how to aid the ex-slaves were transferred without notice. In the Mississippi Valley Confederate forces often launched raids against poorly defended, Union-held plantations, and as a result the freed people suffered much. The army was fighting a war, and its command structure saw military needs as paramount. Freedmen's affairs were a much lower priority, even a distraction or an unwelcome complication. Added to all these factors was the silent but far-reaching influence of racist assumptions among the Northern population. Much went wrong simply because many whites were too busy, too indifferent, or too unconcerned—even when situations were shocking.

Union commanders had promised ex-slave recruits that their families would receive food and shelter. But the army's supply system often failed to provide adequate shelter for the unexpected numbers of ex-slaves. If tents were available, white officers might allow the freed people to use them—at least until military campaign strategy changed and thousands of new soldiers arrived in camp to occupy those tents. The officers who had promised to support the escaped slaves might move on, unexpectedly, to new posts, and then their replacements ignored previous agreements. Frequently promised shelter or wages *never* arrived: on Roanoke Island, North Carolina, wages to black workers went unpaid for three years! One instance, among many, in which the family of a black soldier was evicted from an army encampment received a good bit of publicity because of its tragic consequences. In the midst of an unusually severe stretch of winter weather in Tennessee, the post commander evicted a black soldier's wife and children. One child who was ill died that very day when his mother could not find warm shelter. The mother herself died soon after, and Northern newspapers criticized this incident. But it was only one of many.

There were multiple reasons why, as historian Jim Downs has written, the experience of blacks behind Union lines proved to be toxic. A sympathetic army officer noted that runaway slaves often arrived with little clothing, hungry, exhausted, suffering from disease, or even wounded during their escape. Nevertheless, so many managed to reach Union lines, says Downs, that their flight constituted one of the largest cases of human migration in modern history to that time. Such movement brought together strangers who did not have the same immunities and who now were crowded together amid a shortage of food, shelter, or clean water. In hastily constructed army camps mosquitoes found places to breed, piles of garbage rotted, and human wastes accumulated.

What resulted were explosive epidemic outbreaks that claimed the lives of thousands. These epidemics could not be handled by traditional folk remedies, nor was the army medical service equal to the challenge. It provided little or no care, or unpredictable care, at best. Very late in the four years of war the government created the Freedmen's Bureau, which had its own Medical Division. But even then that division lacked the staff, knowledge, or adequate resources to attack the problems that were killing many newly freed African Americans. In Chattanooga, Tennessee, at the beginning of 1865 black people were dying by the scores. Sometimes thirty men or women at a time lost their new lives in freedom. Army officers had them buried, without coffins, in hastily dug common graves. In Helena, Arkansas, the army carried away black corpses in the same wagons that also carried dead horses and mules. The Democratic newspapers that publicized these problems took pleasure in such antiadministration reports. But supporters of the government, tragically, did nothing effective to solve the problem. There was, in effect, an institutional vacuum that left these fatal problems mostly unattended. They were a heavy counterweight to the progress that was under way.

And the progress was real. Black soldiers were helping the government win the war and preserve the Union. Their service and their valor were doing much to establish freedom throughout the nation. But racism remained deeply embedded in individuals and in society. The struggle for equality clearly had to continue. Though realistic, black leaders were encouraged by the progress that had been made. They brought new determination to their efforts to confront injustice and overcome discrimination.

Notes

1. Quoted in James M. McPherson, *The Negro's Civil War* (New York: Ballantine Books, 1965, 1982, 1991), 313.

2. Ibid., 314.

3. Ibid., 177.

4. Ibid.

5. Ibid., 181–82.

6. Quoted in John David Smith, ed., *Black Soldiers in Blue* (Chapel Hill: University of North Carolina Press, 2002), 235.

7. Ibid., 41.

8. James Henry Gooding, *On the Altar of Freedom*, edited by Virginia M. Adams (Amherst: University of Massachusetts Press, 1991), 39, 40.

9. Quoted in McPherson, *The Negro's Civil War*, 275.

10. Ibid., 279.

11. *New-York Daily Tribune*, June 6, 1863.

12. Quoted in Escott, *Lincoln's Dilemma: Blair, Sumner, and the Republican Struggle over Racism and Equality in the Civil War Era* (Charlottesville: University of Virginia Press, 2014), 166–67.

13. Ibid., 167–68.

14. Quoted in McPherson, *The Negro's Civil War*, 191.

15. Ibid., 242.

16. Ibid., 241.

17. Ibid., 203.

18. Quoted in C. Peter Ripley, ed., *The Black Abolitionist Papers*, volume V (Chapel Hill: University of North Carolina Press, 1992), 305.

19. Quoted in David Williams, *I Freed Myself* (New York: Cambridge University Press, 2014), 1.

20. Congressional testimony quoted in McPherson, *The Negro's Civil War*, 220–26.

21. Quoted in McPherson, *The Negro's Civil War*, 130–31.

CHAPTER FOUR

~

Fighting for Equality

By 1864 African Americans had good reason to be encouraged. The Emancipation Proclamation and the courageous service of black men in the army and navy constituted revolutionary changes—developments unimaginable only a short time before. But there was still much to overcome, much ground to win. Black Americans knew that racism, so long embedded in the nation's culture, had not disappeared. Their legal status remained inferior and uncertain. Even in regard to emancipation, serious questions cast a shadow over the future. Since President Lincoln's proclamation was a war measure, all informed observers agreed that only a constitutional amendment could definitively end slavery. Moreover, if all blacks became free, what would be their status as citizens? The events of war finally were including African Americans in a society that had long excluded them, but what would be their rights, their place in society, the scope of their opportunities? How could they win equality, respect, and human dignity?

Black leaders in the North were determined to gain positive answers to these questions. They took the lead and devoted their energies to this crucial task. Using the advantages they had gained, the skills they had developed, and the relatively privileged position they enjoyed, they used every method to advance the fight for racial equality. Their efforts at the federal level were important, but they also organized and struggled in scores of states, cities, and local communities. The effort to dismantle discrimination had to be local, as well as national, for it was in people's cities, towns, and neighborhoods where racism was active daily, denying hopes and crippling opportunities. Throughout the North, from the Atlantic to the Pacific, black leaders organized and pressed vigorously for progressive change.

A vital theme of all their efforts was a dedication to uplifting and advancing the whole race. Black leaders in the North did not distance themselves from the needs of those in bondage. They identified with all African Americans. They fought for the rights and future of those who had been enslaved as well as those who were free. An emotional and moral identification with blacks living in the Confederacy or laboring within Union lines guided their actions and impelled them to energetic efforts. They sacrificed to support the freedmen, and Southern blacks responded. Joyously they seized opportunities to improve themselves and added their own energies to the effort to seek and demand equality.

1864 proved to be a crucial year, both for the future of black Americans and for the direction of the nation's politics. African Americans made significant progress. Yet before the year was out Northern leaders had to recognize and respond to a political crisis that threatened to turn progress backward. Suddenly a real possibility arose that the Republican Party would retreat from its support for freedom and greater rights. Confronting that danger, black leaders protested, organized, and demanded full equality. More than any other group, they worked with determination to make the United States embrace its founding values and realize its creed.

The black community in the North took seriously its responsibility to lead. Discrimination plagued every area of Northern life for black people, but in the North they could benefit from freedom, the ability to organize, and some opportunities for education. By the time of the Civil War, free blacks had become active in almost every area of business and enterprise. Many individuals owned stores and businesses, had accumulated personal property, and attained an education. Almost two dozen had assets exceeding $100,000, which in those days was accepted as the mark of true wealth. Such individuals, like Philadelphia sailmaker James Forten or Rhode Island's George Thomas Downing, a wealthy restaurant owner, became active in abolitionist activities. Others, like John Mercer Langston or Frederick Douglass, also served the race as lawyers or newspaper editors and lecturers. Ministers often did more than lead and motivate their churches; they also spoke out on public issues.

These efforts had brought significant progress at the national or federal level. In 1861, only four years after the *Dred Scott* decision declared that black people could not be citizens, Henry Highland Garnet, a distinguished minister, educator, and orator, received his U.S. passport. Lincoln's attorney general soon took the position that every person born free in the United States, regardless of race, was a citizen. Congress admitted African Americans to the legislature's galleries, and in 1862 they gained entry to lectures at the Smithsonian Institution. That same year African Americans began to testify in the courts of Washington, D.C., and before the war was over this crucial right extended to all federal courts. Senator Charles Sumner was making progress with his campaign to prohibit the exclusion or segregation of black people by street railways in the nation's capital. Similar efforts were under way to open positions in the postal service to black people. For the first time African Americans met with the president and attended a reception at the White House. Such measures were in addition to the key role of black men in the military service.

As notable as these changes were, they represented only a tiny fraction of the efforts that Northern leaders were making at the state and local levels. A prime example was New York. It was the most populous state in 1860, and its black population may have been the best organized. With the leadership of James McCune Smith, African Americans succeeded in placing on the ballot a referendum measure that would have granted them equal suffrage. To support this proposal, they organized sixty-six local suffrage committees, waged a publicity campaign, and distributed thousands of tracts and pamphlets. Although the referendum failed, their efforts increased the prosuffrage vote.

Fighting for the right to vote was a priority among blacks in every Northern state. Since many states had laws or constitutional language limiting the ballot to "white" men, activists petitioned Northern legislatures to strike this word from the text and allow black suffrage. Other states had property qualifications that excluded many blacks from voting. Northern blacks fought those rules in 1863 in New Jersey, Pennsylvania, Connecticut, Michigan, and Kansas. The black soldier was helping to defeat the rebellion, said Kansas leaders, so he should be a voter to help preserve a restored Union. Although white resistance defeated these efforts, black efforts and the events of the war were building momentum for change.

Northern blacks had more success in other areas. Next to the right to vote, being able to testify in court was extremely important, for without that right any black person was vulnerable to persecution and injustice. As the editor of the *Pacific Appeal* explained, so long as California's statutes "exclude our testimony in courts . . . so long will we be fitting subjects for assaults on our persons and property, by knavish and brutal white men" who know "we have no protection in law."[1] Blacks in California pressed the legislature to change the law, with petitions and public speeches. In 1862, they failed by a narrow margin, but Philip Bell, the newspaper's editor, challenged activists to take defeat as an incentive to try again. The next year, after an even more vigorous campaign by African Americans, the state legislature repealed the rule on testimony. Thereafter, black men could testify in any court case.

In Illinois, John Jones, a prominent black businessman in Chicago, played a key role in efforts to allow black testimony. The law there prohibited African Americans from testifying in any case in which a white person was a party. Jones appealed directly to the governor and the legislature, noting that he paid taxes on property worth $30,000. Forming a Repeal Association, he then broadened the campaign, aiming to do away with Illinois's "black laws." These prohibited entry into Illinois by any black person intending to settle there. The Repeal Association gathered petitions from all parts of the state. Jones himself argued to a legislative committee that blacks deserved the same opportunity as whites, and the lawmakers removed the restrictions. With the exception of Indiana, every other Northern state removed its prohibitions on new black residents and black testimony.

Education was a key to progress in society, and therefore Northern blacks pressed for good, and integrated, schools. A group in Indiana declared that exclusion from the public schools was the worst feature of the black laws. In San Francisco in 1862 other African Americans protested against a school building that was overcrowded and poorly ventilated, with ceilings that were falling down and water dripping onto students' desks. Although the school remained segregated, in 1863 they won construction of a new building. The next year Kansas's lawmakers made local school boards responsible to provide public schools for blacks.

The first battle against segregated schools had been won in Boston in the 1850s. In 1864 Rhode Island's George Downing led a campaign against segregated schools in Providence, Newport, and Bristol. Black Rhode Islanders organized and sent petitions to their local and state governments, and Downing insisted to the governor that "the unholy prejudice against color . . . should die with slavery."[2] When legislators seemed ready to provide equal but separate facilities, Downing and others objected, insisting on integration. Their campaign did not succeed during the war years, but in 1866 segregation in public schools ended in both Rhode Island and Connecticut. Although segregated schools persisted in many of the larger cities of the North, black children attended integrated schools in Michigan, Wisconsin, Minnesota, and the northern parts of Illinois and Ohio.

Another area where African Americans fought against discrimination was urban transit systems. Streetcars in many Northern cities either refused to carry black people or imposed a system of segregated seating. This practice began to change during the war years as a result of sustained protest by African Americans. Black women often took the lead in fighting against this form of discrimination because they depended on streetcars to get to work or church. Without hesitation they stepped out of traditional gender roles to protest, and they were successful. A court decision ended discrimination on San Francisco's omnibus lines in 1864. A war widow brought a legal challenge to New York's streetcars and won that same year. Success soon followed in Cincinnati and in Boston, and by 1864 the major Northern cities had desegregated many railroad lines.

Ironically, Philadelphia—the "City of Brotherly Love"—stubbornly resisted desegregation of its transportation system until after the war was over. But the black abolitionist William Still and others protested discrimination and slowly gained the support of many prominent white citizens. They also petitioned the Board of Railway Presidents and the state legislature. These efforts plus the contributions of black soldiers to the war effort slowly began to change attitudes. By early 1865 a white minister in Philadelphia was outraged when he witnessed two black soldiers ejected from a railway car. He had seen black soldiers fighting and dying on battlefields, and such mistreatment back on the home front was intolerable.

In fighting for their rights, Northern blacks aided their race, but they also were defending the highest values of the nation. They believed in the liberty and equality of the Declaration of Independence and in human brotherhood as taught by the Christian religion. They had no illusions about the hostility that they faced, but they looked forward to a day when they could be fully accepted as citizens and brothers. George Downing told a convention of blacks in New England that God wanted the United States to make brotherhood real. He and others hoped to transform the nation into a place where all belonged and where white and black could work together. Likewise, in wartime New Orleans, editors of that city's *Tribune* assailed efforts to separate Americans along racial lines.

Boston's John Rock once described the task facing black Americans as not just "working our way up in this country" but also "civilizing the whites."[3] Engrained white racism would have to be overcome. Rock and other leaders did not minimize the difficulty of this latter task. They knew, in fact, that demanding their equal political and civil rights was sure to arouse white resentment and fear. Accordingly, black leaders in the North tried to defuse white hostility. They followed a common strategy of drawing a distinction between equal rights and social equality. While they demanded their political rights as citizens, they also tried to disarm racist objections by declaring that blacks were not insisting on close personal relationships with whites.

As H. Ford Douglas told whites of the Western Anti-Slavery Society, "I do not ask you to invite me into your parlors; I ask not to be recognized, socially, by any man in the world. We are not demanding social equality."[4] That would remain a private matter, a question of personal preference. What was essential for African Americans, agreed Frederick Douglass, was "perfect civil, religious, and political equality."[5] On another occasion he insisted that equality meant that all rules for voting should be the same for whites and blacks. In the summary words of John Rock, "All we ask is equal opportunities and equal rights."[6]

In struggling for equality of rights and opportunities, these black leaders thought beyond themselves. Their goal was larger than their own interests or the welfare of free blacks in the North. They also dedicated themselves to the needs and elevation of the newly freed slaves of the South. In a racist nation, racial solidarity defined their goals. America's most privileged African Americans made progress for the least privileged in their cause.

Beyond fighting for freedom and welcoming the Emancipation Proclamation, Northern blacks embraced the monumental challenge of aiding the

Throughout the crisis of the Civil War, John Rock was one of the strongest voices among black leaders. A multitalented man, he was the first African American attorney admitted to practice before the U.S. Supreme Court. Library of Congress, Prints and Photographs Division.

former slaves. The contrabands of 1861 and 1862, and then the freed slaves after 1863, needed both material support and economic and educational opportunity. Hundreds of thousands were entering lives of freedom in impoverished conditions, vulnerable and deprived of all the advantages common to whites. Today we would describe their situation after fleeing from slavery as a humanitarian crisis.

The African Methodist Episcopal Church's newspaper, the *Christian Recorder*, was among the first to make an urgent appeal for aid for the contrabands. Early in 1862 this paper urged Northern blacks to give generously as a Christian act and Christian duty. Clothing, teachers, and relief workers of all kinds were needed. Henry McNeal Turner, pastor of the Israel Bethel Church in Washington, D.C., reminded members of his congregation that their racial identity joined them to the contrabands, whose suffering was extreme. In solidarity and humane sympathy free blacks should "extend a hand of mercy to *bone of our bone and flesh of our flesh*."[7] The *Weekly Anglo-African* affirmed that Northern blacks could best understand the former slaves. The free members of the race, said the paper, were "destined for this work of mercy." For this purpose God had given them some freedom, education, and "the irrepressible desire for equality which consumes our souls." Challenging its readers to take the lead in aiding the freed people, the *Anglo-African* declared that "we will be false to our destiny if we fail to do it."[8]

Thousands of individuals responded. Black carpenter and antislavery activist John Oliver was typical of many. As soon as he heard about the slaves who escaped to Fort Monroe and other places within Union lines, he felt the desire to help. Knowing he could teach, Oliver volunteered in order to give the contrabands an education that would benefit them in freedom. He and others recognized that gaining freedom was only the start of a new life. The former slaves needed a hand up in many ways. Elizabeth Keckley, the dressmaker for Mary Lincoln, was an example of the many who started new relief associations. Members of abolitionist societies organized aid efforts. Others came together in their churches to collect goods and send aid to the freedmen.

Elizabeth Keckley's Contraband Relief Society concentrated on helping the thousands of slaves who escaped to the District of Columbia and Union-occupied northern Virginia. In Boston the Ladies of the Twelfth Baptist Church led the way in gathering donations of money, food, and clothing. In Philadelphia the Mother Bethel Church was very active, and in D.C. Henry McNeal Turner's church established the Union Relief Association. Across the North other churches and voluntary associations sprang into action to aid Southern blacks. Among the most prominent were the Freedmen's

Friend Society in Brooklyn, the Contraband Aid Association of Cincinnati, the Ladies Aid Society of Norwich, Connecticut, and the African Civilization Society of New York. But these are just a few examples of the response that came from black communities across the North. Soon tons of clothing and material aid began to reach Union-occupied portions of the South.

Even more important were the men and women, like John Oliver, who interrupted their lives to go South and help the freedmen. Black volunteers joined with their white counterparts from churches and abolition societies in a massive voluntary effort. The Federal army assigned some officers to use and coordinate this aid, and three organizations played a major role. One of these was the U.S. Sanitary Commission, whose work against disease in army camps included medical care for some of the freedmen. Another was the American Missionary Association, an arm of white Protestant churches, which recruited teachers for the freedmen, including many black teachers. (The American Freedmen's Union Commission, a second missionary association, made similar contributions.) The third was the Freedmen's Bureau, a federal agency established by Congress near the end of the war. As nurses and especially as teachers, Northern black women gave invaluable assistance to the freed slaves.

By the end of 1865 the Freedmen's Bureau had placed more than 1,000 teachers in the South, and over 90,000 first-time students were learning to read and write in 740 schools. In abandoned houses, cabins, tents, or even outdoors, Northern teachers held classes for young black children and for adults. Grown men and women often came to classes at night, after a long day's work, so eager were they to gain an education. Three-quarters of all the teachers were women, and black women were present in disproportionate numbers. Although they were only a very small part of the Northern population, they made up approximately one-eighth of all the teachers. Many of them would continue to work in the South years after the war ended.

Teaching in the South presented real challenges to these idealistic volunteers. Living conditions often were rough or rudimentary. Schools were overcrowded, many of the students were very young, almost babies, and instructional materials were scarce. Teachers faced hostility from Southern whites and endured both loneliness and exposure to unaccustomed diseases. It also was true that teaching in the South meant a considerable cultural clash. The women who volunteered from Northern churches and communities were usually well-educated members of the free black elite. They were highly religious, bent on self-improvement and the attainment of knowledge, social respectability, and high culture. To reach out to former slaves, who had a different culture and had been denied every opportunity, required skills

Throughout the South former slaves rushed to get an education for their children and themselves at schools like this one. Courtesy Library of Congress, Prints and Photographs Division.

of empathy, patience, understanding, and human warmth. Not all the new teachers had these strengths, but many tried to bridge the gap.

One of the best examples of a Northern black woman who met this challenge was Charlotte Forten. Only twenty-four years old when the war began, Charlotte Forten came from a prominent family of black abolitionists in Philadelphia. The wealthy sailmaker James Forten was her grandfather, and as a teenager she had lived in Salem, Massachusetts, with the family of Charles Lenox Remond, another prominent black abolitionist. She had gained a superior education in private schools and at the Salem Normal School, a teacher-training institution. Well versed in English literature, Charlotte Forten began her teaching career in the Salem public schools. Tuberculosis interrupted her teaching in Massachusetts, but after returning to Philadelphia and regaining her health, she began to publish poetry. Then she felt the call to aid the freedmen.

In the fall of 1862, Forten sailed to the South Carolina Sea Islands, aided by the Port Royal Relief Association. When her ship landed at Hilton Head, she caught her first glimpse of the "contrabands." Their appearance was a shock to this elite woman. In her diary she wrote that they were "of every hue and size," though "mostly black." Then she added that they were "certainly the most dismal specimens I ever saw."[9] Her sympathies soon were engaged, however, as some black boatmen rowed her to St. Helena's Island, where she would start teaching. The deep voices of the boatmen impressed her, and she found their songs haunting, sweet, and solemn.

Soon she was busy, teaching classes of various sizes and various ages. Before the year was out she had as many as fifty-eight students in her class, including quite a few young children. She called the youngest her tiny ABC pupils, because they were too small to learn more than the alphabet. It was difficult and stressful to manage such a large class, but Forten found that many of her students were both eager to learn and bright. She wanted to give them a good basic education but also reasons to feel proud of their race and hopeful about the future. Consequently, she made sure to tell them about John Brown, Northern abolitionists, and various black heroes, such as Toussaint L'Ouverture, the "Black Napoleon" who had led the revolution against slavery in Haiti. Forten's teaching included night classes for various adults, whose eagerness to learn often outstripped that of the students.

For this upper-class, cultured woman from Philadelphia and Salem, Massachusetts, the religious services of the former slaves seemed primitive and backward. She regarded New England decorum as a mark of civilization. Therefore she described the first "shouts" she witnessed as a "barbarous expression of religion, handed down to them from their African ancestors, and destined to pass away under the influence of Christian teachings." With time, however, she learned to appreciate the enthusiasm of the former slaves' worship. She admitted to being amused by some of the "headdresses" women wore, which she thought ridiculous. But when she saw couples' eagerness to enter into legal marriage, she overlooked the women's headdresses and praised "the poor creatures" for "trying to live right and virtuous lives." Daily conversation taught her about the harsh realities of slavery, as when one woman described 1862 as a very happy year. "Nobody to whip me nor drive me," she said. "[P]lenty to eat. Never had such a happy year in my life before."[10]

Forten also appreciated the natural warmth and generosity of these former slaves. Their gratitude touched and impressed her, for they tried to repay her for everything she did for them. She praised the progress of her eager students in a long, two-part essay that was published in the *Atlantic Monthly*. On the Sea Islands, she wrote, slavery had conspired to create the most "degraded negroes of the South," yet she witnessed men, women, and children working hard to improve themselves. She also seized the opportunity of this article to send a message to prejudiced whites. "One cannot believe that the haughty Anglo-Saxon race, after centuries of such an experience as these people have had, would be very much superior to them," she concluded. "And one's indignation increases against those who, North as well as South, taunt the colored race with inferiority while they themselves use every means in their power to crush and degrade them, denying them every right and privilege, closing against them every avenue of elevation and improvement."[11]

Charlotte Forten and the Southern freed people were different in culture and life experiences, but Forten's work and her diary entries prove that she had a deep commitment to her entire race. In this she exemplified the North's free black community. The relative liberty and privilege that had enabled progress for Northern blacks did not alienate them from those who had suffered under bondage. Discrimination and white hostility taught them all that they were one people. A very special group, the successful light-skinned Creoles of New Orleans, had quickly reached the same conclusion. Although they had enjoyed a status superior to slaves in the very diverse, multiracial society of New Orleans, they devoted themselves to advancing the interests of all Louisiana's black people and became leaders for the race.

Like their Northern counterparts, the leaders in New Orleans pressed for the right to vote. President Lincoln had been encouraging the organization of a loyal, pro-Union government in the occupied portions of Louisiana. This so-called "ten-percent" government, formed because at least 10 percent of Louisiana's prewar voters participated, wrote some antislavery measures into law. It declared emancipation throughout the entire state and established public schools that would include blacks as well as whites. It also drew up a constitution that would permit the legislature to give black men the right to vote. However, the legislature failed to act. In protest, leaders of New Orleans's free black community traveled to Washington and gained an audience with the president. "We are men; treat us as such," they told him.[12] Lincoln was so impressed with their bearing and eloquence that he wrote to Louisiana's governor and made a private suggestion—that the legislature give the right to vote to some black men. He suggested including very intelligent men and soldiers who had fought gallantly for the Union. Unfortunately, Louisiana's white lawmakers still refused to act.

Two months later, in May 1864, the American Freedmen's Inquiry Commission spoke out for black rights. This commission had already predicted that the former slaves would outgrow the negative influences of slavery and become useful members of society. Now it called for an equal and color-blind system of justice and the guarantee of political and civil rights. Arguing that the former slaves were the most loyal people in the South, the commissioners declared that freedmen must have equal rights in order to protect themselves and to protect reconstruction. With equal rights, their votes could assure that reconstruction would be permanent and peaceful. Two members of the commission then published books insisting on the freed people's right to vote. One of the three members, James McKaye, also raised the idea of including Southern blacks in a redistribution of lands, based on confiscated estates or abandoned plantations.

The *Weekly Anglo-African* believed that land was essential to the future progress of the South's slaves. As early as 1861, an editorial in this important black newspaper asked "What Shall Be Done with the Slaves?" Focusing on economic advancement, the editor predicted that during the conflict "lands will be confiscated to the government, and turned into public lands." Four million former slaves, "accustomed to toil, who have by their labor during sixty years past supported themselves, and in addition, an extravagant aristocracy," would need a way to make a living. With convincing reasoning, the editor asked, "What course can be clearer"—as well as more just, humane, and beneficial to the public interest—than the idea "that the government should immediately bestow these lands upon these freed men who know best how to cultivate them?" Not only would the distribution of such lands "restore the equilibrium of commerce," but it also was morally right. These were "lands which they have bought and paid for by their sweat and blood."[13] Boston's John Rock agreed, saying that the nation owed compensation to the former slaves. They should have land in the South, land that was theirs by right of long labor and suffering.

John Rock and the *Weekly Anglo-African* correctly understood the views and attitudes of the South's freed slaves. An elderly man from the Sea Islands explained why land ownership was important to him. He wrote to President Lincoln, explaining, "If we colored people have land I know we shall do very well."[14] A black man from North Carolina added that land should be the "inheritance of the Americans of African descent." They had earned it "through a life of tears and groans."[15] The black editors of the *New Orleans Tribune* agreed with this moral argument: "the land tillers are entitled" to "soil they have so long cultivated. . . . If the Government will not give them the land, let it be rented to them."[16] Army officers noted that almost all the slaves longed to have a little land so that they could establish their own farms and homes.

Land and the ballot were two vital questions. They went straight to the heart of African Americans' possibilities for economic advancement and political influence, and they would be of crucial importance at the end of the war and in Reconstruction. Before the war ended, however, and before the Union could claim victory, African Americans confronted a crisis in the summer of 1864 that threatened to roll back much of the progress they had made.

1864 was a pivotal year, both for the Union and for African Americans. The war was not yet won, and the preservation of the Union remained in doubt. The future of African Americans depended upon a Northern victory, but also upon legal changes to make freedom permanent and to confer rights long denied. The outcome depended not only on events on the battlefields but also on the regularly scheduled presidential and congressional elections. Would Abraham Lincoln be reelected, or would he be replaced by some other candidate? Would the Republican Party gain strength to advance freedom, or would a Democratic Party sympathetic to the South come into power?

Black leaders in the North knew that they had to agitate for continued progress and counter any attempts to roll back reforms. Their pressure could help to make a difference, so they paid close attention to the candidates and issues. Far from Washington, African Americans in the South also were following the war's events and watching for opportunities that could benefit their progress. Despite the disadvantages of distance and education, they often developed a shrewd and insightful understanding of events and the developments that mattered most to them.

When Northern black activists first looked toward the 1864 elections, many saw reasons to be grateful and loyal toward Abraham Lincoln. Brooklyn's J. W. C. Pennington made the case for supporting Lincoln in a letter to the *Weekly Anglo-African*. Looking back over the country's history, Pennington called Lincoln the only president who had paid attention to the concerns of African Americans. Because Lincoln was honest and hated by both the rebels and their Northern sympathizers, he urged Lincoln's reelection. "The wisest, the safest, and the soundest policy," he thought, would be to reelect the president, so that the "well-begun work of Negro freedom and African redemption will be fully completed."[17]

In far-off San Francisco, a mass meeting of blacks endorsed Lincoln at the beginning of the year, and the *Pacific Appeal* joined in his praise. Lincoln, said the newspaper, had defied the slave power and defended the status of black people as citizens. Through his acts as commander-in-chief he had given military protection to African Americans. Moreover, his plans for Reconstruction had called for education for the freedmen. Philadelphia's Robert Purvis and other leaders pointed to a substantial list of progressive steps. These included: the abolition of slavery in the District of Columbia, the prohibition of slavery from the territories, suppression of the international slave trade, recognition of Liberia and Haiti, and of course the Emancipation Proclamation and the enrolling of black men in the army. Happy that the government no longer supported slaveholding, Purvis expressed his gratitude to Lincoln.

Yet even Purvis admitted that the government was not fully committed to freedom and equality, and other leaders were more critical of the nation's chief executive. They recalled how often Lincoln's actions had lagged behind the steps taken by Congress. They remembered the way he had overruled two generals who proclaimed emancipation, the support he frequently voiced for colonization, and his failure to act effectively to end discrimination against African American soldiers. Even the Emancipation Proclamation had given slaveholders a chance to reenter the Union and keep their slaves, a fact that the *Pacific Appeal* and others denounced. One subscriber to the *Weekly Anglo-African* saw Lincoln's policies as uncertain and changeable. The president endorsed antislavery one day and colonization the next, and he always gave concessions to slavery when possible. The *New Orleans Tribune* touched on another sore point when it recalled the way Lincoln had urged black leaders in Washington, D.C., to take the lead in colonization. Lincoln seemed to blame African Americans, not white racism, when he told them that, except for the presence of black people in the nation, white people would not be killing each other.

As long as Lincoln was the only possible progressive candidate, many Northern black activists were willing to blame his shortcomings on the white population whose support he needed. But as the nominating conventions neared, another candidate entered the field. John C. Frémont had ambition and, seemingly, the progressive credentials to attract considerable support. In 1856 he had been the first presidential nominee of the Republican Party, and he had been the first general to try to decree emancipation. Now abolitionists and a portion of the Republican Party, consisting of so-called Radical Republicans who were dissatisfied with Lincoln's conservatism, rallied to his support. They announced the formation of a Radical Democratic Party and scheduled a convention that met in Cleveland late in May 1864. There they nominated Frémont for the presidency and wrote a platform that called not only for a constitutional amendment abolishing slavery but also for another step forward: complete equality before the law.

This platform excited many who wanted faster and greater progress against slavery and prejudice. To an abolitionist and advocate for women's rights like Elizabeth Cady Stanton, Lincoln had failed to measure up. Radical Republicans in Congress felt that he had held them back, forcing them to make progress in spite of him. The chairmen of some important Senate committees wanted another nominee. For some black leaders, too, the Frémont candidacy and platform were very appealing. Frederick Douglass wrote a public letter endorsing the new party. Frémont gained Douglass's endorsement because he stood for the ending of every form and legacy of slavery throughout the nation. His support for equality in the courts, at the polls, on the battlefield, and in every state went beyond what Lincoln had done.

The Republican Party, when it held its convention, did not go as far as Frémont's Radical Democratic Party. Lincoln was renominated, and the party called for the passage of a constitutional amendment to prohibit slavery. But it took no position demanding stronger measures or equality before the law in every respect. Still many black leaders were relatively happy to remain in the Republican camp. They reasoned that Lincoln was not free, politically, to do everything they wished he would do. Considering the depth of white racism in the electorate, they were willing to credit Lincoln and the Republicans for accomplishing a lot.

Then, in July, some unexpected events raised serious questions about Lincoln's plans and even about the Republican Party's commitment to complete emancipation. These events forced black leaders—at the very moment they were assembling to plan the next steps forward for equal rights—to protest and bring all the pressure they could to bear on the president. Suddenly they had real cause to fear that progress might go backward.

By July the war-weary Northern public was eager for peace and an end to the war. Only with the benefit of hindsight can we see, today, that the Union armies were moving inexorably toward victory. Then, military affairs seemed deeply discouraging. General Sherman's army was somewhere in Georgia, moving slowly toward the railroad junctions at Atlanta, but no breakthrough had occurred. Meanwhile, in Virginia, the news was awful and awfully discouraging. General U. S. Grant, vowing to keep the pressure on the Confederate army of Robert E. Lee, attacked repeatedly. But the battles were bloody, extremely costly, and never decisive. It seemed that almost every day the newspapers carried long lists of the killed, maimed, and missing. Despite huge loss of life, no end—no victory—seemed to be in sight.

Then Lincoln made a political mistake that hurt him with the white electorate. For African Americans, his next steps were positively alarming. The president's efforts to recover ground with whites showed where his priorities were and caused profound concern and fear among black leaders.

Confederate President Jefferson Davis had sent to nearby Canada three commissioners, who put out the word that they wanted to talk about peace. Under pressure to at least explore that possibility, Lincoln issued a public statement. In a letter headed "To Whom it may concern," he declared on July 18, 1864, that he would consider "any proposition which embraces the restoration of peace, the integrity of the Union, and the abandonment of slavery." Such an offer would have to come from "an authority" empowered to end the fighting.[18]

Suddenly there was an outcry from wide segments of the war-weary Northern public. The Union's goal, critics insisted, had always been to preserve the Union. Lincoln and the Republicans had justified all their antislavery actions as necessary measures to win the war and restore the Union. Why was the president now adding emancipation as a precondition to peace talks? Democrats and their newspapers jumped on Lincoln's words, which they pictured as a shocking change and an unjustified "ultimatum." The *New York Herald*, for example, demanded to know why Lincoln had taken this new, extreme ground. Always before he had insisted that preserving the Union was most important. More racist newspapers charged that he was planning to squander white lives without limit and impoverish the country, all to elevate the status of the undeserving Negro. Even Republican editors reacted with surprise and criticism.

As attacks such as these multiplied, Republicans leaders gauged public opinion and despaired. Leaders of the party in state after state agreed that Lincoln had blundered. The incoming chairman of the Republican National Committee bluntly told the president that his support was evaporating. The lack of military success was a serious problem, but now, in addition, the public believed that he was insisting on the controversial step of emancipation before there could be peace.

Facing such a crisis, Lincoln and his allies looked for a way out, for some verbal formula that could save their political fortunes. Lincoln himself drafted a letter that contained a clever, face-saving formula. The evasive argument that he invented was that his promise to consider peace *with emancipation* did not mean that he would *refuse* to consider *something else or something less*. Lincoln then consulted with various people, including Frederick Douglass, on whether he should send this letter. Douglass, of course, objected strongly, and ultimately Lincoln put his draft in a drawer. But that did not stop his allies and his party from making the argument.

The Republican *New York Times*, for example, energetically pushed these ideas for him. The *New York Times* insisted that Lincoln had "never 'refused to receive or consider any proposition looking to peace or Union unless accompanied with the abandonment of slavery.' He has never 'prescribed' that abandonment as a 'sine qua non' of receiving or considering such propositions."[19] Papers like the *Albany Evening Journal* joined in this effort, and Secretary of the Interior John Usher repeated the same formula in a public address. Secretary of State William Seward defended Lincoln with words that raised additional concerns for African Americans. Seward said the war would stop immediately once rebels laid down their arms, and then courts and legislatures could take up the remaining issues. Seward's vague and worrisome formula even became part of Lincoln's annual address to Congress.

But what, exactly, did all this evasion and backpedaling mean? The answer clearly was: nothing good for black rights. Suddenly, winning reelection seemed more important to Lincoln and his allies than insisting on freedom for the majority of the slaves. The Republican Party's commitment to emancipation had never been total, and many leaders, including Lincoln, had denied that they were abolitionists. Now the promise of freedom for millions of African Americans was about to be traded away for partisan electoral advantage.

These startling developments occurred at a crucial time for the North's black leaders. They were coming together in Syracuse, New York, in the most important convention they had ever planned. Since the 1830s, leading African American activists had been meeting in conventions to share information and advice and to identify ways to advance the race. Their organization was called the National Convention of Colored Men, although the delegates in 1864 included two women: Edmonia Highgate, a teacher among the freed slaves; and Frances Ellen Watkins, a writer and lecturer.

Two thousand spectators and 145 voting delegates arrived in Syracuse from all parts of the North east of the Mississippi and even from eight Southern states. They had to brave white violence in many of the cities they passed through, but they received support from black churches and were welcomed into many black homes.

Leaders of the national convention had planned an agenda that would totally reject colonization and look ahead to the end of the war. They wanted to develop specific plans for advancing the rights of all African Americans during the process of Reconstruction. Now these new developments would have to claim the attention of the delegates and alter their agenda.

Frederick Douglass was elected the convention's president, and he summed up the delegates' basic and long-standing purpose. They met to promote the freedom and progress of the race, to gain full citizenship and the right to vote, and to help their people advance in knowledge, civilization, and influence. In recognition of the sacrifices made by black troops, the convention hung the battle flag of the First Louisiana Colored Troops across the platform and praised their bravery at Port Hudson. The sacrifices of black soldiers in saving the Union would constitute a strong claim for that crucial right, the right to vote on the same terms as white men.

But swiftly the convention moved to address all that had happened in response to Lincoln's "To Whom It May Concern" letter. Alert to all the dangers that it posed, the delegates mounted strong protests. Frederick Douglass named the fear felt by other delegates when he told the body that an immediate peace without full and official destruction of slavery could mean that the status of colored people would remain unchanged. These leaders had to speak out. The need to challenge the Republicans and pressure them to do the right thing strongly shaped the final address of the convention to their fellow citizens in the Union.

After surveying the injustices long suffered by black Americans, their address criticized the Republican Party as still influenced by "contempt for the character and rights of the colored race." It recited every hesitation or weak measure of which the Republicans were guilty before the summer. Then it indicted what was worse: after the reaction to Lincoln's letter, it was "very evident that the Republican party . . . is not prepared to make the abolition of slavery, in all the Rebel States, a consideration precedent to the re-establishment of the Union." Even more serious was Secretary Seward's speech, whose "studied words . . . mean that our Republican Administration is not only ready to make peace with the Rebels, but to make peace with slavery also."[20] The administration was backing away from the destruction of slavery. Seward and Republican newspapers were in agreement that all actions against slavery by Congress and the president would stop as soon as the rebels laid down their arms. Congress thus far had refused to propose a constitutional amendment prohibiting slavery, and the convention had little faith in the Supreme Court. What, then, could end human bondage in America—only the madness of the rebels, if they continued to fight until their society was destitute and all their slaves were free.

Resolved to carry these protests back to their homes, the delegates also took important steps to support present progress and to build a better future. They praised the successful efforts of the organizations that were giving material and educational aid to the freed slaves. They pledged to work for the interests and advancement of the freed people and promised to do all they could to help. In addition they demanded the ballot for Southern blacks, warning that if freed slaves were not allowed to vote, they would suffer from the resentment, wrath, and fury of defeated Southern whites. Most importantly, the delegates founded the National Equal Rights League. This new organization was designed to have great importance in 1865 and beyond. Through its local, state, and national chapters it would carry forward the fight for full equality, for equal rights under the law, and against segregation and exclusion from public schools and facilities.

Lincoln made no response to the protest, but his electoral crisis eased in September. Two things saved the president's reelection: military success and the missteps of John C. Frémont. Most important was the breakthrough accomplished by General Sherman's army. On September 2, Sherman's men captured Atlanta, a result that brought joy to the North and spread gloom through the South. That important victory convinced most people in both sections that the Union would, indeed, win the war. Then a number of errors by John C. Frémont derailed his rival candidacy. Though nominated by radical antislavery men who wanted a stronger policy than Lincoln's, Frémont went too far in courting Democratic votes and alienated his original supporters. He withdrew from the race on September 21. The candidate of the Democratic Party, George C. McClellan, was anathema to almost all Republicans and certainly to black leaders.

Boston's John Rock expressed the views of many when he declared, "There are but two parties in the country to-day. The one headed by Lincoln is for Freedom and the Republic; and the other, by McClellan, is for Despotism and Slavery."[21] Frederick Douglass repented of his interest in Frémont shortly before the latter withdrew as a candidate. Douglass explained that when it had seemed possible to elect "a man . . . of more decided anti-slavery convictions and a firmer faith in the immediate necessity . . . of justice and equality," he had withheld his support from Lincoln. But "that possibility is now no longer conceivable," and a victory by the hostile Democratic Party was completely unacceptable.[22] Robert Hamilton, the publisher of the *Anglo-African*, acknowledged that Lincoln had not done all he could against racial oppression. "[B]ut that is not the question now. . . . if you are a friend of liberty, you will give your influence and cast your vote for Abraham Lincoln."[23]

These sentiments were shared by Radical Republicans, who swallowed their objections and campaigned hard for the president. Black soldiers, like James Ruffin, who was stationed in South Carolina, pulled for the president's reelection. "We are all for Old Abe," Ruffin wrote to his sister. "I hope he will be elected. Let the colored men at home do their duty."[24] Southern slaves and freed people were also following developments in the North's election with more insight than many would have assumed possible. Although they could not vote, black men in Nashville held a mock election and favored Lincoln over McClellan by 3,193 votes to 1. The Northern electorate moved in the same general direction. After Sherman's victory in Georgia, most white voters in the North felt more encouraged, and soon the tide turned in Lincoln's favor. He won reelection and urged Congress to propose the Thirteenth Amendment to end slavery.

African Americans then looked ahead. As Northern leaders organized to work for greater progress once the war ended, Southern blacks focused on the practical steps that would do the most to advance their lives in freedom. The record shows that many of them had a clear and well-informed understanding of how the war's issues had developed in the North. They also faced the future with a realistic, sober, but also hopeful understanding of what should be done in the South. A telling example of the political knowledge of Southern blacks surfaced at the end of 1864, after General Sherman had marched through Georgia.

On December 21 Sherman took Savannah. He then settled into the city for a few months, resting his troops and preparing for a new campaign northward through the Carolinas. There was pleasure over Savannah's capture, but also interest and scrutiny directed Sherman's way due to his attitudes toward black troops and his treatment of some escaped slaves during his march through Georgia. Early in the new year Secretary of War Stanton visited Sherman to confer, to examine the general's policies, and to interview black leaders. The members of the American Freedmen's Inquiry Commission also had been interviewing black Southerners about slavery and freedom. Their findings matched the information that came out of a meeting with General Sherman.

Twenty local black leaders met with the Northerners and answered a series of questions. These black men ranged in age from twenty-six to seventy-two; five had been born free, several had previously been freed by their owners, and most had gained freedom during the war. All were ministers or teachers and lay officers in area churches. They relied on one man, Garrison Frazier, to be their primary spokesman. Frazier was sixty-seven years old, a longtime Baptist minister who had bought himself and his wife eight years before. His answers to questions about the coming of the war and the politics of emancipation revealed a shrewd and realistic insight about white people and the future.

Reverend Frazier and his companions understood that the war did not begin to free the slaves but because the South rebelled. The North's initial purpose was only to defeat the rebellion and preserve the Union. They also understood that Lincoln tried, through his Preliminary Emancipation Proclamation, to induce the Confederates to lay down their arms and end the rebellion. If they had come back to the Union by January 1, 1863, they would have been able to keep their slaves. The fact that they did not end the rebellion made freedom for the slaves a part of the North's war aims. In summarizing these facts, Frazier demonstrated that he and his colleagues had a clear understanding of both Northern public opinion and the limits of the Republicans' antislavery convictions.

With General Sherman present, Frazier interpreted the general's military success as fulfilling a purpose ordained by God. After Sherman had left the room, he did not attack the general but declared that he had treated the black leaders with courtesy. Frazier assured the secretary of war that thousands of freed blacks were ready to enlist, despite the fact that Union officers sometimes coerced black men to join the army. Many former slaves were eager to meet the slaveholders in combat; others were willing to support the army in its quartermaster or commissary departments. All the freed people, Frazier said, overwhelmingly supported the U.S. government. If all their prayers for the Union were known, it would take weeks to read through them.

Asked what freedom for the slaves meant, Frazier defined it as having the chance to earn pay from their labor, to support themselves, and to help the government in maintaining their liberty. He declared without hesitation that the South's former slaves could take care of themselves. Calmly answering a question that revealed the common prejudices of many whites, he declared that, yes, Southern blacks were intelligent enough to survive under the equal protection of the laws and were able to maintain good relations among themselves and with Southern whites. But Reverend Frazier demonstrated both his hopes and his realism about the South and Southern whites when he was asked how the freed people could best live in the days ahead.

"The way we can best take care of ourselves is to have land," he said. "We want to be placed on land until we are able to buy it and make it our own." Frazier accurately described the desires of his people; the officers who commanded black troops everywhere saw that former slaves wanted to have a little land and a home of their own. Frazier also captured the feelings of many freed people when he was asked if they wanted to settle among the white population or be separate in black communities. "I would prefer to live by ourselves," he replied, "for there is a prejudice against us in the South that will take years to get over."[25] Only one of the nineteen men who accompanied him disagreed.

This meeting had a remarkably positive and encouraging outcome. General Sherman also was probably thinking of a way to avoid having slaves flock to his army and accompany him on his march into the Carolinas. For whatever combination of reasons, Sherman soon issued Special Field Order Number 15. In this order Sherman decreed that the islands and coastal areas that had been abandoned by Southern slaveholders—from Charleston, South Carolina, to the St. Johns River in northern Florida, and for thirty miles inland from the coast—should be set aside for settlement by freed slaves. Black families could have a forty-acre plot and enjoy the protection of the U.S. army. Congress would have to decide whether the land would remain theirs permanently.

Thus, 1864 was a year that showed the determination and energy of black leaders. It also showed the unity and solidarity of African Americans in the face of continued challenges. Those who had previously been free never forgot the men and women in bondage. Instead, they organized and worked to aid and educate the freed people. At the same time they continued to agitate for equal rights and opportunity in all parts of the nation. They made progress, and they protested against the Republican Party when its support wavered. In all these efforts African Americans demonstrated that they were the best exemplars of the values of the Declaration of Independence. Still, they confronted a nation whose white majority remained hostile or indifferent. The end of the war did not mean that their lives would suddenly become easy.

Notes

1. Quoted in James McPherson, *The Negro's Civil War* (New York: Ballantine Books, 1965, 1982, 1991), 254–55.

2. Ibid., 271–73.

3. Ibid., 83.

4. Quoted in C. Peter Ripley, ed., *The Black Abolitionist Papers*, five volumes (Chapel Hill: University of North Carolina Press, 1992), V: 94.

5. Quoted in McPherson, *The Negro's Civil War*, 289.

6. Quoted in Ripley, ed., *The Black Abolitionist Papers*, V: 305.

7. Quoted in McPherson, *The Negro's Civil War*, 136.

8. Quoted in Ripley, ed., *The Black Abolitionist Papers*, V: 176.

9. *The Journals of Charlotte Forten Grimké*, edited by Brenda Stevenson (New York: Oxford University Press, 1988), 388.

10. Ibid., 419, 391, 393, 397–99, 396, 402.

11. Quoted in Lewis C. Lockwood, ed., *Two Black Teachers during the Civil War* (New York: Arno Press and *New York Times*, 1969), 71.

12. Quoted in Paul D. Escott, *Lincoln's Dilemma* (Charlottesville: University of Virginia Press, 2014), 209, 198.

13. Quoted in McPherson, *The Negro's Civil War*, 297–98.

14. Ibid., 301.

15. Ibid., 298.

16. Ibid., 299.

17. Quoted in Ripley, ed., *The Black Abolitionist Papers*, V: 276–77.

18. Quoted in William E. Gienapp, ed., *This Fiery Trial* (New York: Oxford University Press, 2002), 201.

19. Quoted in Paul D. Escott, *"What Shall We Do with the Negro?": Lincoln, White Racism, and Civil War America* (Charlottesville: University of Virginia Press, 2009), 133.

20. *Minutes of the Proceedings of the National Negro Conventions, 1830–1864*, edited by Howard Holman Bell (New York: Arno Press and *New York Times*, 1969), 1864—Syracuse, Proceedings of the National Convention of Colored Men, 12–13, 57, 48, 50–52, 34, 25.

21. Ibid., 24.

22. Quoted in McPherson, *The Negro's Civil War*, 310.

23. Ibid., 311.

24. Ibid., 311.

25. Sherman Meets the Colored Ministers in Savannah, January 12, 1865, http://civilwarhome.com/shermanandministers.htm.

CHAPTER FIVE

~

Facing a Difficult Future

As 1865 began, African Americans sensed that the Civil War would end soon. A Union victory was in sight, and with it came many reasons for them to feel optimistic. In less than four years, the war had brought remarkable change. In fact, progress had seemed to gain momentum as time passed. The Emancipation Proclamation led to black soldiers joining the army, where their courage and sacrifice strengthened their claim to citizenship. Northern black leaders won the repeal of some discriminatory laws in many localities and organized themselves for greater progress. Republicans in Congress had taken steps toward equality, with laws addressing unequal pay for troops and freedom for soldiers' families. Then the lawmakers began consideration of a constitutional amendment to prohibit slavery and established the Freedmen's Bureau. In the South the Union army had steadily extended its area of control. Schools began to reach more and more freed people. Lastly, Sherman's Special Field Order Number 15 gave hope to many former slaves that economic independence would be possible in the postwar years.

North or South, African Americans were not naïve about their situation and prospects. They had endured too much oppression to ignore realities. They knew that they remained a minority, denied the right to vote, in a white democracy where racism was deeply rooted. The political maneuvering by President Lincoln and his allies, in reaction to the electoral scare caused by his "To Whom It May Concern" letter, showed that progress for black Americans was not the administration's highest priority. They recognized that the struggle for freedom and equality was far from over. Protests, petitions, and pressure remained essential for African Americans to overcome society's racism. But there seemed good reasons to be encouraged.

Then unexpected tragedy cast doubt over the revolutionary changes that had started to dismantle old fortresses of slavery and racism. The assassination of Abraham Lincoln in April shocked the entire nation and deprived African Americans of a leader who had done much to advance their cause. The North, tired of war and eager to return to the comforting routines of peacetime, hoped for reassurance and stability from a new president. But African Americans wondered if Lincoln's successor, Andrew Johnson, had their welfare at heart. A Southerner and a former Democrat, his attitude toward the freedmen and black rights was in doubt, and his record as Lincoln's wartime governor of occupied parts of Tennessee was not encouraging. In 1862 he had even convinced Lincoln to exclude Tennessee from the Emancipation Proclamation.

Thus, as the war ended, African Americans saw that clouds were gathering over their future. Northern blacks had reason to fear that the federal government was losing interest in their progress. Southern blacks encountered abundant evidence of white prejudice and hatred. There would be new challenges and new difficulties as African Americans sought to advance the agenda of freedom. The war years had meant struggle and sacrifice for them. The postwar period was going to be no different. But as the war ended, African Americans in all parts of the nation showed that they were ready for the challenge. Their actions in defense of their rights demonstrated a determination to continue fighting in the long battle to gain equality.

At the beginning of 1865 the newspaper of the African Methodist Episcopal Church, the *Christian Recorder*, reflected on the status of the African race. Compared to their position at the beginning of the war, black Americans had made rapid strides. The paper's editor saluted them on their moral, social, and political advances. In the army, he said, former opponents had admitted and praised blacks' valor, courage, and manhood. The military prospects for a Union victory were favorable. Looking to the future, the editor declared that further efforts to achieve the goals of universal freedom and racial justice were necessary.

The war and black protest were bringing important changes that undermined and dismantled the institution of slavery. But because the Emancipation Proclamation was a war measure based on military necessity, change in fundamental laws and constitutions was necessary to make it permanent. As 1865 arrived, this occurred in two of the four slaveholding states that had remained in the Union. Both Maryland and Missouri had been exempt from the Emancipation Proclamation, and therefore slavery had remained legal there. But it came under increasing criticism in both states. First Maryland held a state constitutional convention that proposed the abolition of slavery. The work of that body won approval by the state's voters, and slavery ended there in October 1864. Similar events were occurring in Missouri, and by the end of 1864 politicians who favored immediate, rather than gradual, emancipation gained the upper hand. A state convention voted for immediate emancipation in Missouri in January.

Even more encouraging and more important was the action of Congress that same month. President Lincoln sent a special message to Congress, whose members would remain in office only a few more weeks before newly elected lawmakers took their seats. This "lame duck" Congress had failed, by a narrow margin, to support a proposed Thirteenth Amendment to abolish slavery throughout the nation. After the Republican victory in the fall elections, Lincoln now argued, the passage of this proposed constitutional amendment by the next Congress was virtually assured. In the interests of unity during the national crisis, he called on Congress to act—to approve the amendment and to send it to the states for ratification. Members of his administration lobbied individual congressmen with every means at hand, including the application of political pressure and various personal inducements. They succeeded, and at the end of January 1865, Congress approved the text of the Thirteenth Amendment. The end of slavery, after more than two centuries of legal existence, was now very close.

To celebrate this historic event, Republicans in Washington arranged for a public religious service that would, itself, be historic. For the first time in the national experience, an African American would speak from the floor of Congress. Reverend Henry Highland Garnet, pastor of the Fifteenth Street Presbyterian Church in Washington, D.C., agreed to deliver the sermon. Garnet was the son and grandson of slaves and had been born into bondage. When he was a child, his parents escaped from slavery, and he then pursued every opportunity to gain an education. As he matured, he became a distinguished pastor, abolitionist, and activist for black rights. Garnet seized this occasion not to celebrate what was achieved so much as to challenge white and black Americans to make greater progress.

He took as his text Jesus's criticism of the scribes and Pharisees—prominent, intelligent, and well-informed men who "knew their duty but did it not." In the United States such people had been the leaders of the nation, even leading men from liberty-loving New England. He denounced their long indifference to slavery, and then described the cruelty and wickedness of bondage itself. With many learned allusions, as was the custom in oratory of that day, Garnet attacked "the sin of slaveholding" and the failure of the nation's founders to do anything about it. Congress's recent action finally gave promise that the "gigantic monster," slavery, would perish. But next it was necessary "that all unjust and heavy burdens should be removed . . . all invidious and prescriptive distinctions should be blotted out from our laws," and that all men should "enjoy every right of citizenship." African Americans should have not only the right to vote but also the right to be equal before the law "in every respect" and free "to make [their] own way in the social walks of life." He challenged the Christian churches to discard "caste and prejudice" and called on the nation to atone for its sins. He ended his sermon with a call to "*Emancipate, Enfranchise, Educate, and give the blessings of the gospel to every American citizen.*"[1]

While Northern black leaders, like Henry Highland Garnet, were pushing for more progress, the freed people of the South were acting on their own to secure full freedom and equal rights. Early in January 1865, blacks in Tennessee petitioned the leaders of their state to treat them justly. A loyal government was being formed in Tennessee, and a Union Convention was meeting in Nashville to draw up a new constitution. That constitution, declared the fifty-nine black men who signed the petition, must expressly abolish slavery. If it did not, masters would make every effort to put their former slaves back into bondage. Freedom, insisted the petitioners, was a natural right, and the sacrifices of black troops in preserving the Union reinforced their claims for justice.

With good political instincts, they also pointed out that black Tennesseans could be counted on to support the Union party in postwar politics. Therefore "negro suffrage" would be politically helpful as well as just. If "the Government has asked the colored man to fight . . . it can afford to trust him with a vote." The right to testify in the courts also was an essential legal protection, and they asked their "white brethren" to let them share in developing the state.[2] These arguments were heard, at least in part. The new constitution ended slavery and barred any compensation for slaveholders. It did not, however, grant African Americans the right to vote.

Other parts of the South were not so advanced in reconstituting loyal governments, a process that had to wait for the end of the war. But the freed people were working to better their condition in every practical way. As families and as individuals, they took advantage of the possibilities that their escape from slavery had given them. One of the most important goals for former slaves was to gain legal recognition and protection for their marriages, something of fundamental importance that had been denied them in slavery. In the army and with the help of the Freedmen's Bureau, African Americans rushed to legalize their marriages. In Arkansas, for example, they kept an army chaplain busy almost every day of the month. After the painful separations imposed by slavery, they were eager to make their marriages legal and official. It meant a great deal to have their weddings documented in a record book furnished by the U.S. government. For men and women who had been living together for years, as well as for younger couples, the legal and religious importance of marriage was vital.

Northern army chaplains, who often had some prejudiced assumptions about the slaves, applauded this evidence of a desire for social respectability and moral virtue. But the former slaves wanted to prove their fitness for full-fledged citizenship. The Tennessee freedmen who petitioned their state's legislature, for example, emphasized that "We know the burdens of citizenship, and are ready to bear them. We know the duties of the good citizen, and are ready to perform them cheerfully."[3] The same was true in Richmond, Virginia, where three thousand freed people crowded into the First African Church and listed their claims to civil responsibility. With 20,000 black people in the area, "more than 6,000 of our people are members . . . of Christian churches" and nearly all "attend divine service. Among us there are at least 2,000 men who are worth $200 to $500; 200 who have property valued at from $1,000 to $5,000, and a number who are worth from $5,000, to $20,000." Despite slavery's laws against education, "3,000 of us can read, and at least 2,000 can read and write."[4]

The hunger of ex-slaves for an education continued to grow. As a group near Falls Church, Virginia, put it, they wanted to be able to give their children a good education, and therefore it was essential to have a schoolhouse located in a central, convenient spot. Wherever Northern missionary associations or the Freedmen's Bureau opened a school, African Americans appeared in great numbers, young or old. In addition, Southern blacks made remarkable efforts to provide education for themselves through subscription schools. By paying as much as a dollar per month, black families with very little income recruited teachers and hired them to give education to thousands of black children. The Freedmen's Bureau later reported that about half the schools for blacks in the South were supported by such subscriptions. There was the same enthusiasm for learning in the army. An officer attached to a black regiment from Louisiana reported the rapid gains in education by the men of his unit. Despite carrying out their military duties with increasing efficiency, the soldiers had made marked progress in learning to read and write. In only a year, troops who had been almost entirely illiterate were now almost universally gaining the rudiments of an education.

With an acute grasp of economic and social realities, Southern blacks focused much of their attention on the need for land, once they were free.

They wanted land in order to build their own homes and operate independent family farms. They understood that without land they would be dependent once again on the former slaveholders. Moreover, in a nation where most of the citizens were farmers, owning a farm was the obvious path to full membership in the economy and society. In a South filled with defeated and angry whites, owning land would be a powerful source of economic security and social independence. Taking advantage of Sherman's Special Field Order Number 15, forty thousand African Americans quickly settled on plots along the southeastern coast and began working them as family farms. In the Mississippi Valley, where the Union army had control of many abandoned plantations, former slaves hoped they might gain land. All these developments sustained the optimism that African Americans had reason to feel in the closing months of the war.

One of the most joyous moments for some of the South's slaves came at the beginning of April 1865. As General Grant's army closed its military vice around the badly outnumbered forces under General Robert E. Lee, the Confederate government fled from its capital. With the city under the control of the Union army, an exhausted and underweight, but gratified, President Lincoln decided to visit Richmond in person. On April 4 he and his twelve-year-old son, Tad, began walking through the streets of Richmond. It was Tad's birthday, and he and the president were in high spirits.

But their happiness could not compare with the joy and excitement Richmond's black population showed. Grateful African Americans surrounded Lincoln as he and Tad walked through the city. They celebrated the defeat of the Confederacy, and with shouts and applause they showed their gratitude to the president who had done much to bring this about. Some shouted blessings to the president, while others threw their hats in the air. In response Lincoln asserted that "liberty is your birthright. . . . it is a sin that you have been deprived of it for so many years." But he also voiced a condescending white attitude when he told the freed people, "You must try to deserve this priceless boon. Let the world see that you merit it, and are able to maintain it by your good works."[5]

Everywhere that African Americans were free or within the reach of the Union army, there was similar jubilation. In Washington, D.C., on April 3, when news of the fall of Richmond arrived, excited crowds, both black and white, poured out into the streets. One week later General Lee's army surrendered, and the celebration was, if possible, greater. Churches rang their bells, flags flew in front of homes and stores, and as night fell candles and gas jets illuminated almost every building in the nation's capital. African Americans shared in all this excitement. Not only was the long war over, but the slaveholding Confederacy was defeated. The end of slavery now seemed even more certain.

The very next day, April 14, Lincoln was shot. By the morning of April 15 he was dead. The act of Lincoln's assassin, John Wilkes Booth, had everything to do with race. Booth, a well-known actor who felt it was his sacred duty to aid the Confederacy, had witnessed Lincoln's last public address. On April 11 the president had spoken to a happy crowd that had gathered outside the White House. His prepared remarks covered a variety of topics but focused on Reconstruction. He had defended his ten-percent government in Louisiana, which did not allow any African Americans to vote but had established public schools for blacks and whites. He also had said, in regard to the right to vote, that he would prefer giving the ballot to "the very intelligent [black men], and on those who serve our cause as soldiers." Hearing those words, Booth "was enraged. 'That means nigger citizenship,' he said. 'Now, by God! I'll put him through. That is the last speech he will ever make.'" When Lincoln attended a play at Ford's Theatre, Booth delivered on his threat.[6]

The entire nation was shocked. A heavy atmosphere of fear and sorrow hung over the capital. Many people closed themselves up in their houses, as if they expected another great calamity and feared for the future. Where Lincoln's body rested in the East Room of the White House, huge crowds slowly filed past to pay their respects and have a last look at the president's face. Many men and women wept. Even in the South there were defeated Confederates who felt that they had lost a fair-minded executive who might have treated them with sympathy.

African Americans, however, had the deepest reasons to mourn. Black leaders had criticized Lincoln's hesitations and shortcomings and pressured him to do more. Still, in a nation that long had treated them cruelly and unjustly, he was their best-known symbol for a belief and faith that progress was possible. On Hilton Head Island in South Carolina, freed people assembled and drew up resolutions of sorrow. They called Lincoln's death a national tragedy and an immeasurable loss. They praised their "beloved President" for his "wisdom and Christian patriotism" and for the Emancipation Proclamation that proclaimed "*Liberty* to our race." The *New Orleans Tribune* honored Lincoln as the "benefactor of our race," and a black soldier stationed in Charleston considered his loss "irreparable. Humanity has lost a firm advocate, our race its Patron Saint, and the good of all the world a fitting object to emulate."[7]

In Washington, D.C., hundreds of African Americans defied a cold rain to stand for hours in front of the White House. During a long day the number of black mourners remained steady and strong. Women and men, and families with their little children, showed their respect for the president who had presided over important changes. Surely they wondered, as well, what the future would bring now that the author of the Emancipation Proclamation was dead.

Such worrisome doubts and fears proved to be all too appropriate during the rest of 1865. With the war's end, the character of public sentiment changed, and the government entered a new phase in its political life. The Civil War had been a time of unremitting crisis—four years of uncertainty, bloodshed, sacrifice, and a constant sense of emergency. It was in that tense and exceptional atmosphere that unexpected change and progress occurred. The evolution of decades seemed to have been compressed into a few months or a year. Even the leaders of the government marveled at how rapidly they had discarded old expectations and beliefs in order to adapt to the crises of war. Like the ordinary citizens, they had changed their lives and their thinking under the pressure of an emergency situation. But now that emergency was over, and a desire for stability and life's comforting, familiar patterns reasserted itself. The public wanted to escape from crisis and return to normal times.

In politics this feeling translated into a widespread hope in the North that Lincoln's successor, Andrew Johnson, would govern well and wisely. White voters seemed willing to give him a substantial and tolerant trial in hopes that he would continue Lincoln's policies, act reasonably, and avoid new disruptions. The first order of business was Reconstruction. The nation would have to be reunited by bringing the defeated Southern states back into the Union. Here the realities of race and past history worked against African Americans. Before the years of crisis, the United States had always been a white-majority nation that sanctioned slavery and discrimination. The Southern states that now claimed the government's attention were predominantly white, hostile to any form of black progress, and resentful in defeat. Would the North's white majority favor Southern whites over the interests of black Americans who, except for a few states in New England, could not even vote? Political realities and past practice seemed to weigh in the South's favor.

In addition, it turned out that the first crucial decisions rested with Andrew Johnson. The Northern Congress adjourned in April, and its members would not return to Washington until December. During that long interval Johnson began the process of Reconstruction and made choices that would greatly disadvantage African Americans. With his cabinet he discussed the question that Lincoln had raised in his last public address. Should the freedmen, or any of them, enjoy the right to vote? When the cabinet split evenly on this issue, Johnson decided that he would call for new Southern governments based solely on white voters. The defeated Confederate states would have to hold constitutional conventions, but only white men would vote and frame the new state governments. Thus, Johnson gave defeated Southern whites the power to make decisions. No sooner had the Civil War ended than black leaders, North and South, learned that they would have to fight for future progress, or even to retain the gains that they had made during the war.

Despite disappointment, they responded to the challenge. In petitions and resolutions from various parts of the South, the freed people showed that they were both determined and politically insightful. Showing a clear understanding of the methods and processes of democracy, they came together in meetings and conventions. These were efforts to influence the agenda and an implicit challenge to the undemocratic, white-only conventions authorized by President Johnson. They also were the only practical means for freed people to fight for their rights and seek the benefits of liberty.

Men who had been free before the war often took leadership roles in these assemblies and conventions. The fact that many of them had been able to gain an education increased their usefulness for the entire group. But uneducated former slaves from rural areas also were well represented. Even in South Carolina, where urban blacks formed the largest part of the delegates, those from rural districts made up 40 percent of the freedmen's convention. Working together, these leaders—whether former slaves or formerly free, urban or rural, mixed race or fully black—confronted a daunting task. They encountered many varieties of the continuing racial oppression that was general throughout the former Confederacy. Some delegates had to travel at night to be safe. Others appealed to the military authorities for safe-conduct papers in hopes of preventing attacks. In different states blacks used different strategies to try to win changes from unsympathetic white leaders. Their knowledge of America's democratic values and procedures was impressive, and they made their case well. But the task that lay ahead of them would prove formidable and discouraging.

In North Carolina more than one hundred black leaders from across the state met in Raleigh, the state capital. There they drew up an address to the white constitutional convention that Andrew Johnson had called into being. Their strategy was one of respectful persuasion. In a well-written address, they put forward a variety of appeals to the convention's delegates. Admitting that President Johnson's policy gave them no power to control legislation, they made a "moral appeal to the hearts and consciences of the people of our State." They reminded lawmakers of their "obedient and passive" behavior during the war, when they had aided the Confederacy by building fortifications and raising food on farms and plantations. Shrewdly they recalled the "intimacy of relationship" fostered by slavery and declared "we have formed attachments for the white race which must be as enduring as life."[8] As North Carolinians, they planned to stay at home and prove their importance to the state through hard work, sobriety, and constructive behavior. They even acknowledged that Federal troops would not stay in the South much longer to protect them from mistreatment. Instead they declared that they wanted to merit fair treatment by contributing to the state as valuable citizens.

But after making this respectful case for favorable consideration, the North Carolina blacks spoke out against injustice. Some landowners had tried to keep their slaves in bondage. Others had driven workers away without paying them, or forced women and children to leave just because their husbands had died. The black leaders called for education, respect for the sanctity of marriage, fair treatment as laborers, and clearly defined work hours. They welcomed the boon of freedom and wanted "all the oppressive laws which make unjust discriminations on account of race or color wiped from the statutes of the State." Appealing to the whites' self-interest, they sought support in elevating themselves, arguing that "our longer degradation cannot add to your comfort, make us more obedient as servants, or more useful as citizens." Theirs was an eloquent and strong argument for fair treatment, "friendly relations," and "mutual co-operation."[9]

Sadly, but not unexpectedly, the constitutional convention of North Carolina rejected these reasonable arguments. In fact, its members took great offense that free blacks and former slaves had dared to present such a petition. Instead of hearing their pleas, it denounced them for offensive boldness. Then North Carolina, along with the other states in the South, proceeded to draw up laws known as "black codes" that restricted the rights and liberties of the former slaves.

In this discouraging setting, South Carolina blacks spoke out, strongly yet in a spirit of "patriotic good-will." Fifty-two delegates met in Charleston's Zion Church, where they composed a protest and appeal. Invoking religion, the Golden Rule, and the Declaration of Independence, they sought justice. Through generations of slavery, laws that "made white men great have degraded us." Now they called for "*even-handed Justice*" and the rights of citizenship.[10] They protested against black codes that barred them from testifying in court, voting in elections, and engaging in legitimate businesses without expensive licenses or other handicaps. They argued the need for schools for their children and the opportunity to buy land. Though slavery had held them back, these African Americans were proud of the progress they had made. Through their address to the people of South Carolina, they called for an equal chance under the law to better themselves.

In Kentucky African Americans faced an even more complicated and discouraging situation. Slavery remained legal in Kentucky, since it had not seceded, and as national approval of the Thirteenth Amendment drew closer, that state's slaveholders had become ever more hostile. Therefore, several black leaders took their protest directly to the president. Kentucky, they said, was "the only Spot" in the United States "where the People of color Have No rights *whatever* Either in law or in fact." Without the protection of the military, Kentucky's black population would feel "four fold the Venom and Malignanty" of slaveholders and white mobs.[11] In Louisville, for example, a city councilman who previously had ordered guards to whip black people on the city streets now was trying to remove all military protection. It was essential, said the black leaders, that martial law continue in force. In addition to living under state laws supporting slavery, black Kentuckians could not testify in court, own a home, move about freely, or defend themselves. The state's legal code prescribed imprisonment for any free man of color who visited, even briefly, in a free state. Free blacks from other states, if they entered Kentucky, were subject to the same penalty and could be sold into slavery for a second offense. Yet thirty thousand black Kentuckians had fought to preserve the Union. Their leaders called for the security provided by Federal forces in order to avoid relentless oppression.

Hostility toward the freed people was common all over the South immediately after the war's end. Defeated Confederates were bitter and tenaciously opposed to change. A Northern journalist who spent fourteen weeks traveling through the Southeast found a great deal of resentment toward Yankees and African Americans. There was an almost universal feeling among whites that blacks must be kept in their place. There was even less willingness to accept any new status as free people and citizens. Some planters who previously had boasted of their attentive concern for their slaves now said that free blacks were worthless and that they wanted to be rid of them.

In South Carolina the whites talked obsessively about the Negro and claimed that almost all freed slaves soon would want to return to the care of their former masters. Without white control, they claimed, black people would not work and therefore would be unable to survive. One former slaveholder bluntly explained that landowners needed to whip their black laborers. Yet this man considered himself a very kind master and was shocked that his slaves fled as soon as Union troops entered Charleston. In rural districts some whites feared that the former slaves might stage an uprising, a fear that made them even more inclined to harshness. The leaders of the Freedmen's

Bureau wanted to help the freed people. But many low-level officers in the Freedmen's Bureau seemed completely unfit for their duties.

In Georgia a Northern journalist found only a few instances in which African Americans could get reasonable wages. In those cases the farm work was going well, and both landowners and laborers were prospering. But white Georgians were determined that race relations should be left up to them, and their idea of proper race relations was to preserve white supremacy in every area. Consequently, the freed people had to be suspicious and on guard against the whites. Even more frequently than in South Carolina he heard whites claim that former slaves would never work now that they were free.

West of the Mississippi River, the situation was different but no more encouraging. Many slaves were still waiting to enjoy their freedom. Since 1863 the Confederate government had been cut off from the Trans-Mississippi states. News was slow to cross the Mississippi River and slower still to reach remote areas. The main Confederate army in the region did not surrender until the beginning of June. Tens of thousands of slaves did not learn, officially, that they were free until the latter part of June 1865. Only then, or weeks later, could they begin to enjoy the protection of the Federal army or the assistance of the Freedmen's Bureau.

It was on June 19 that a Union general arrived in Galveston with orders to take control of Texas for the Union. He promptly made a public declaration that all slaves were free. Immediately the African Americans in Galveston began to celebrate and spread the word. But even then some slaves probably did not hear official words until a few weeks later. The delayed notification in Texas is the reason that today, among many African Americans, emancipation celebrations take place on June 19, instead of January 1.

Elsewhere in the South, some landowners tried to keep the news of freedom from their slaves. This tactic worked best in areas that were extremely rural, but the semideveloped character of the Southern economy meant that many farms remained quite isolated. Other slaveholders turned to a different tactic in order to maintain control over their former slaves. Using the local white courts, they made "apprentices" of black children. If the white-dominated courts apprenticed black children to their former owner, the children's parents had to remain on the plantation too, in order to be a family. Thus, even where freedom had arrived, some African American families were not able to enjoy it.

Among many disappointments at the end of the war, the greatest probably concerned land. Forty thousand freed people who had gone to work on the lands set aside by General Sherman were shocked to learn that President Johnson had decided to restore all the land to its former owners. A dignified but deeply felt protest from African Americans on Edisto Island exemplified the anguish of thousands of others. Writing to General O. O. Howard, head of the Freedmen's Bureau, they said, "We want Homestead's; we were promised Homestead's by the government." They argued, too, that if the government took their lands away, their condition would be worse than in slavery. General Howard had counseled forgiveness after the war, but whites who still used the whip and denied all opportunities to their former slaves were showing no forgiveness. The whites wanted to keep blacks in "a condition of Helplessness." Saying "We have not been treacherous," these former slaves predicted that "the state will make laws that we shall not be able to Hold land even If we pay for It." Without land, homes, or votes, the freed people could "only pray to god & Hope for *His Help, your Influence & assistance*."[12]

General Howard lacked the power to overrule the president, but he pledged to ask Congress to defend the former slaves' rights. Howard believed they were wise to want homesteads, and he was confident they could hold any lands they had already purchased. But since few sales had actually occurred, he could only advise the people of Edisto Island to accept contracts with white landowners and to work for wages. If they could accumulate some

Emancipated slaves, like these on Edisto Island, South Carolina, longed to obtain land, which could be the basis of an independent life in freedom. Courtesy Library of Congress, Prints and Photographs Division.

money, perhaps they would be able to lease or purchase land in the future. He also suggested that they petition Congress.

Instead of going to Congress, they sent another eloquent petition directly to the president. In a respectful but strong manner, they reminded Johnson that "secession was born and Nurtured" by Southern planters and that "we were the only true and Loyal people that were found in possession of these Lands." After fighting *for* the Union, why, they asked, would they have fewer rights than those who fought to *destroy* it? They sought "the privilege of Purchasing land. . . . We are ready to pay for this land When the government calls for it." They prayed to God that they would not again find themselves at the mercy "of those who have cheated and Oppressed us for many years. . . . We wish to have A home if It be but A few acres. Without some provision is Made, our future is sad to look upon . . . [even] dangerous."[13] But the blessings of God that they wished upon the president did not touch his heart or change his policies. And thus African Americans saw that the war, even if it brought liberty, would not bring them rights and opportunity. Continued struggle against white opposition, persistent and redoubled efforts to overcome racism and discrimination, would be required both North and South.

Fighting oppression in the South, as the war came to an end, was a constant, daily, interpersonal matter. Under Andrew Johnson and his policies, former slaveholders and other whites resisted black freedom at every step. The freed people did their best to avoid conflict. Throughout the South they invited cooperation from whites. For example, on the Fourth of July blacks in Raleigh, North Carolina, marched with a banner reading, "With malice toward none, with charity for all." In New Bern, North Carolina, a mass meeting declared that the freed people had no intention of stirring up conflict. Such displays were similar to the tone of petitions and declarations elsewhere. But instead of finding cooperation, African Americans usually met with hostile resistance.

Landowners cheated black workers out of their wages and whipped men and women as they did under slavery. Former slave owners retaliated against black people who no longer had to obey their every command. In Tennessee freedmen from one county protested that some brutal whippings involved four or five hundred lashes. In parts of North Carolina officials struck black citizens in the street, simply for walking free or using the sidewalk. Without the ability to testify in court, black people were vulnerable to this abuse and had no means of redress. In Virginia, when a black soldier returned home to reunite with his wife and children, his former owner cursed him for fighting against the Confederacy, told him that slaves were not free, and refused to let him see or bring away his family.

As records of the Freedmen's Bureau show, the freed people encountered white violence simply for being free. Any actions that were not subservient put them at risk. Blacks had to complain to the bureau to gain any support. In typical cases, two boys reported being whipped; and a woman complained about her employer, who struck her and refused to give her anything to eat. Others faced eviction from farms, without pay, after they had worked for months to raise a crop. With shocking frequency, blacks told about assaults and shootings. Many whites simply refused to accept that black people were free, and landowners told their workers that they never could be free. The Freedmen's Bureau tried to rein in the abuse of black Southerners and was the closest resource for freed people. But many officers of the bureau tried to satisfy both parties, often by admonishing blacks against normal actions that whites called impertinence.

As a result, blacks resisted the demands and injustices of the whites in hundreds of practical ways. Individuals refused to tolerate any more whipping. One woman informed her former master that he was not going to punish her children anymore. When a former mistress struck another freed woman, she grabbed the white woman's leg "and would have broke her neck." Everywhere the freed people resisted cruelty and resolved not to take "more foolishness off of white folks."[14] They complained to the Freedmen's Bureau about nonpayment of wages, unfair distribution of the harvest, or personal mistreatment. They also claimed the normal and ordinary rights of free people. Some left work to go to a religious revival that was important to them. Others put caring for a spouse who had fallen ill above following the landowner's demands. When obtaining land was impossible, they held out for decent wages. Landowners who offered low wages or expected to continue the routines of slavery found that their workers had gone on strike. Rice planters often discovered that their former slaves no longer were willing to work under the difficult and unhealthy conditions of a rice plantation.

In every rural area the freed people were making decisions whether to leave or stay on the plantations where they had been slaves. They wanted to work where they would have the best chance of improving their lives and making progress in freedom. With that in mind, the freed people judged the character of their former owners. Most former slaves continued to work for owners who had been comparatively good in the days of slavery. But wherever a slaveholder had been cruel, almost all the black people left. A woman from Louisiana who had suffered under a cruel master explained that none of the slaves wanted to stay with that man. Some former slaves in North Carolina who had endured mistreatment also left quickly, but first they told their old master exactly what they thought of him. The desire to reunite with a spouse or family member who lived elsewhere determined some decisions. Other blacks moved to towns or cities, where they could see more of their race, enjoy military protection, escape white supervision, or find better opportunities for employment.

A crucially important benefit of freedom for many blacks was the chance to search for long-lost family members. Slaveholders had broken up many families by selling slaves or giving one member of a family group to a relative who might move far away. The disruptions of the war and service in the army also had separated many husbands and wives, parents and children. In freedom African Americans set out on quests to find loved ones, no matter how difficult or impossible the task seemed. Some walked long distances, even traveling through several states. Many continued searching for years. To obtain promising leads, all relied on the goodwill and local information that other blacks gave them. These searches would have seemed hopeless but for the fact that often they succeeded. Freedman Bryant Huff recalled when his former owner sold Bryant's father and broke up their family. On the day of the sale, Bryant's father vowed that he would return, whether it took months or years. He told his wife to wait for him, and she refused to marry again and grieved over his departure. Somehow, at the war's end, Bryant's father found his way back to his family.

Despite all that former slaves could do personally and on their farms or in their neighborhoods, the chance for real opportunity was going to depend on national politics. The hostility and prejudices of Southern whites, resentful now over their defeat in the war, were simply too great for blacks in the South to overcome. The resistance to treating freed people with basic human dignity was enormous, and few if any Southern whites were willing to give blacks any of the rights of citizenship. Radical Republicans, abolitionists, and black activists would need to influence politics and change the national agenda. The North's desire to return to normal conditions, and its willingness to trust in Andrew Johnson, would have to end. Progress toward real freedom and equal rights needed to begin again, without the benefit of a war-driven emergency.

Black leaders in the North were ready to take up this challenge, despite their small numbers and limited influence. They threw themselves into the task and worked to secure equal rights for Southern blacks and African Americans in every state. The National Equal Rights League now was in existence, and before half of 1865 had passed blacks had organized nine state leagues. The national office was small and limited in staff. It depended on donations from local activists and the state branches, and these often had committed the bulk of their resources to local campaigns. But the national office could provide coordination, share information, and bring leaders together annually for a national convention. The state leagues were more active because they were in direct contact with ordinary black citizens and directly engaged with local problems.

These state leagues pushed forward on battles that had begun during the war years. In 1865 they had a few successes and demonstrated a staying power that could lead to more. The public schools in Chicago and in some smaller cities of the North were desegregated by the end of 1865. In Rhode Island's campaign against school segregation, George Downing and others rejected a compromise in 1865 that claimed to provide equal access to separate schools. But they would prevail in the state legislature the next year. The long effort against discrimination in Philadelphia's streetcars made progress in 1865, as a committee of influential whites tried to negotiate with the streetcar company. Neither the company nor the Democratic mayor would agree to change, so black leaders carried their effort to the state legislature. Although it would take two more years, they eventually gained a state law barring all discrimination in public transportation throughout Pennsylvania. Another encouraging milestone in a depressing year was the admission of Boston's John Rock to argue cases before the U.S. Supreme Court. Though Rock was only one individual, his new status stood as a rebuke to the *Dred Scott* decision. Only eight years before, that same high court had declared that no African American could be a citizen of the nation.

Every local victory was important, but it was clear that black people would have to renew the struggle and carry their campaign for equal rights, justice, and dignity into Reconstruction and beyond. The first annual meeting of the Equal Rights League, held in Cleveland in the fall of 1865, showed that they accepted this difficult task. Forty-one delegates were present on the first day, and a few more arrived before its business was completed. John Mercer Langston, a leading abolitionist and lawyer from Ohio who later would be the first dean of Howard University Law School, served as president. Other prominent black activists at the meeting included George Vashon, William Forten, and James Rapier, who had been born in Alabama and had been active in Tennessee. Eight of those in attendance in Cleveland came from Southern states. President Langston began the meeting with a call for closer union between African Americans in the North and the South.

Acting on President Langston's concern, the delegates thoughtfully discussed the situation of the freed slaves and passed several resolutions about their future. The league declared that as a part of any Reconstruction program, Southern blacks must have the right to vote. It also approved a proposal from the Pennsylvania chapter that called for a constitutional amendment to prohibit, everywhere in the nation, laws that discriminated against any group on account of race or color. Speaking directly to the former slaves, the delegates urged them to focus on acquiring property, educating their children and themselves, and proving by their deeds that they were entitled to a respected place in society. The delegates pledged to give their support to these efforts and declared that it was vitally important that black men and women staff Southern schools. To make that happen, they called on well-educated African Americans in the North to volunteer for teaching positions.

The belief that black Southerners must be taught by black teachers arose from a realistic awareness of the depth of American racism, rather than from any desire for separation. The leaders meeting in Cleveland had seen too much evidence of the retreat from progress to trust even white allies. Near the beginning of the meeting James Henry Harris, a well-educated leader from North Carolina, bluntly spoke out about some unpleasant truths. "White men are white men, the world over," he declared. Given white racism, African Americans could not rely on the morality or goodwill of whites. Instead, he told the delegates, the "elevation of the Negro depends on his own right arm."[15] Philadelphia's William Forten also spoke frankly about the shortcomings of white leaders. He blasted the Republican Party for promising much, for inviting and welcoming the sacrifice of black soldiers, and then failing to give black men the ballot. He noted also, with dismay, that some Republicans still favored colonization or the establishment of some separate territory where black people would live by themselves.

Forten and the other delegates all rejected colonization or emigration. They passed a resolution opposing any movement to colonize members of their race in Africa or anywhere else. Black Americans wanted to gain and enjoy their full rights in the United States. They demanded the ballot, equal political rights of all kinds, and equality before the law. Their determination remained what John Rock had named some years before: to remain in the United States and to reform the country and its white residents—in short, to help the nation live up to its ideals.

That demanding task lay ahead for African Americans. Their experience in the Civil War had brought stupendous gains. Slavery, an institution whose economic importance was vast and whose influence on social life was fundamental, finally came to an end. Many cities and towns had removed some discriminatory laws. Black leaders had made the right to vote and equality before the law an unavoidable part of the national debate. African Americans could feel satisfaction that they had played a major role in bringing about these very important results.

This gallery of important black leaders includes many of those who were influential during the Civil War, plus a few who became prominent in the postwar period. Library of Congress, Prints and Photographs Division.

But to gain the destruction of slavery, they had paid a high price. In battle, in contraband camps, and in crowded army outposts, thousands had suffered and died, while all encountered harsh discrimination. Some rejoiced at the attainment of long-sought goals. Many others saw their health and their dreams of a better life shattered. The price of freedom had been high, but African Americans readily paid that price to gain liberty and equality. Then, as the Civil War ended, the possibility of rapid progress toward equality receded into the distance. To gain their rightful place in America, a long, tiring struggle lay ahead. The goal of equal rights and equal treatment, under a government founded on ideals of liberty and equality, still lay in the future. Achieving equality would demand the work of generations. Even today it remains our national challenge.

Notes

1. http://archive.org/details/memorialdiscourse00garn is the site for Garnet's Memorial Discourse.

2. Quoted in Ira Berlin, Barbara J. Fields, Steven F. Miller, Joseph P. Reidy, and Leslie S. Rowland, eds., *Free at Last* (New York: New Press, 1992), 1, 498–99.

3. Ibid., 499.

4. Quoted in John David Smith, *We Ask Only for Even-Handed Justice* (Amherst: University of Massachusetts Press, 2014), 19.

5. Quoted in Paul D. Escott, *Lincoln's Dilemma: Blair, Sumner, and the Republican Struggle over Racism and Equality in the Civil War Era* (Charlottesville: University of Virginia Press, 2014), 207.

6. Ibid., 211.

7. Quoted in James M. McPherson, *The Negro's Civil War* (New York: Ballantine Books, 1965, 1982, 1991), 311–12.

8. The Address by a Convention of Black North Carolinians is in Sidney Andrews, *The South Since the War* (Boston: Ticknor and Fields, 1855), 128–31.

9. Ibid.

10. Address of the Colored State Convention to the People of the State of South Carolina, Zion Church, Charleston, S.C., November 24, 1865, quoted in http://historymatters.gmu.edu/d/6514.

11. Quoted in Berlin et al., *Free at Last*, 406–8.

12. Committee of Freedmen on Edisto Island, South Carolina, to the Freedmen's Bureau Commissioner, the Commissioner's Reply; and the Committee to the President, October 20 or 21, 1865, October 22, 1865, and October 28, 1865, quoted in online document, http://www.freedmen.umd.edu/Edisto petitions.htm.

13. Ibid.

14. Quoted in Paul D. Escott, *Slavery Remembered* (Chapel Hill: University of North Carolina Press, 1979), 144.

15. *Proceedings of the First Annual Meeting of the National Equal Rights League* (Philadelphia: E. C. Markley and Son, 1865), 4 online at http://babel.hathitrust.org/cgi/pt?id=hvd.hnvpf5;view=1up;seq=10.

~

Documents

Black Leaders Resist the Discouraging Events of the 1850s

Slavery seemed to be gaining ground all through the 1850s. African Americans were especially concerned about the Fugitive Slave Law of 1850, the Dred Scott decision of 1857, and their lack of rights in the courts. H. Ford Douglas was a fugitive slave who had been born in Virginia, but in the free states he became an energetic abolitionist who demanded equal rights. In 1860 he was living in Illinois, where he was unafraid to speak out in criticism of the shortcomings of abolitionists or the weak measures of Republicans. Here he criticizes the inaction of presidential candidate Abraham Lincoln and his Republican colleague, Illinois Senator Lyman Trumbull.

H. Ford Douglas Speaks to the Western Anti-Slavery Society

September 23, 1860

The Republicans say they are bringing the Government back to the policy of the fathers. I do not desire to do this; the policy of the fathers was not uncompromising opposition to oppression; and nothing less than a position far higher than they occupied will ever make us worthy of the name of freemen. . . . We are in fellowship with slaveholders, and so long as we remain in this position we are no better than they. The receiver is as bad as the thief. When you consent to carry out the fugitive slave law, you do as badly as to hold slaves. . . . Yet Abraham Lincoln will carry out the fugitive slave law, and you will carry him into office! He will be the bloodhound to catch the slave, and send him back to his hard life of toil, and you by sustaining him, will make yourselves as guilty as he. I want to see the day when no slaveholder will dare to come here for his slave. But that day cannot come so long as you are willing to exalt to the presidency men who endorse the Dred Scott decision. And all your presidential candidates do this. I know this has been denied of the Republican candidate. But does anyone who hears me deny that Abraham Lincoln endorses even the worst features of that infamous decision, "that the black man has no rights which the white man is bound to respect"? If anyone denies or doubts it let him speak. In the state of Illinois, I cannot testify against a white man in any court of justice. Any villain may enter my house at Chicago and outrage my family, and unless a white man stands by to see it done, I have no redress. Now, I went to Abraham Lincoln, personally, with a petition for the repeal of this infamous law, and asked him to sign it, and he refused to do it. I went also to Lyman Trumbull, with the same petition, and he also refused; and he told me, if I did not like the laws of Illinois, I had better leave the State! This is the doctrine of the Dred Scott decision in its most odious form. It is declaring, not only in words, but in action, the infamous principle that colored people have no rights which you are bound to respect. And yet, you tell me, you are anti-slavery men, while you support such men as these for the highest offices of the nation! . . .

I do not come among you, as a colored man, to ask any special favor at the hands of the white people; I ask only that my manhood be recognized before the law—only that you shall repeal your unjust enactments against the colored race. I do not ask you to invite me into your parlors; I ask not to be recognized, socially, by any man in the world. We are not demanding social equality. All we ask is the same rights, legally, as yourselves, and to grant this is as necessary to your own well-being as to ours. When our rights are recognized, and let our merits decide the rest.

Source: C. Peter Ripley, editor, *The Black Abolitionist Papers*, five volumes (Chapel Hill: University of North Carolina Press, 1992), 5: 91, 92, 94.

Runaway Slaves Begin to Change the Agenda

In the first days of the war three slaves—Frank Baker, Shepard Mallory, and James Townsend—escaped across Chesapeake Bay and arrived at Fort Monroe. They took risks not only in escaping from the Confederates but also in turning themselves in to Union officers, who usually were sending fugitive slaves back to their masters. However, these men were able to tell Fort Monroe's commander, General Benjamin Butler, about the Confederate defenses on which they had been working. They were eager to help the Union army instead, and this caused Butler to consider keeping runaway slaves as "contraband" of war and using them in support of the Northern cause. These three men showed Northerners that slaves could aid the Union while simultaneously subtracting support from the Confederacy. Here General Butler explains the reasoning that eventually prevailed in U.S. policy.

Commander of the Department of Virginia to the General-in-Chief of the Army

[*Fortress Monroe, Va.*] May 27 /61

Sir

(Duplicate)

. . . .

Since I wrote my last dispatch the question in regard to slave property is becoming one of very serious magnitude. The inhabitants of Virginia are using their negroes in the batteries, and are preparing to send the women and children South. The escapes from them are very numerous, and a squad has come in this morning to my pickets bringing their women and children. . . . I have . . . determined to employ, as I can do very profitably, the able-bodied persons in the party, issuing proper food for the support of all, and charging against their services the expense of care and sustenance of the non-laborers, keeping a strict and accurate account as well of the services as of the expenditure. . . . As a matter of property to the insurgents it will be of very great moment, the number that I now have amounting as I am informed to what in good times would be of the value of sixty thousand dollars. Twelve of these negroes I am informed have escaped from the erection of the batteries on Sewall's point which this morning fired upon my expedition as it passed by out of range. As a means of offence therefore in the enemy's hands these negroes when able bodied are of the last importance. Without them the batteries could not have been erected at least for many weeks As a military question it would seem to be a measure of necessity to deprive their masters of their services How can this be done? As a political question and a question of humanity can I receive the services of a Father and a Mother and not take the children? Of the humanitarian aspect I have no doubt. Of the political one I have no right to judge. I therefore submit all this to your better judgement, and as these questions have a political aspect, I have ventured—and I trust I am not wrong in so doing—to duplicate the parts of my dispatch relating to this subject and forward them to the Secretary of War.

. . . .

Benj. F. Butler

Source: Benj. F. Butler to Lieutenant Genl. Scott, 27 May 1861, B-99 1861, Letters Received Irregular, Secretary of War, Record Group 107, National Archives. Published in Ira Berlin, Barbara J. Fields, Steven F. Miller, Joseph P. Reidy, Leslie S. Rowland, editors, *Free at Last: A Documentary History of Slavery, Freedom, and the Civil War* (New York: New Press, 1992), 9–10.

Growing Numbers of Slaves Escape into Union Lines

Everywhere that Union forces advanced, slaves seeking freedom poured into the Northern army's lines. The exodus started by Frank Baker, Shepard Mallory, and James Townsend could not be stopped. During the first two years of the war slaves gained an opportunity to flee only around the edges of the Confederacy, where the Union army made advances on the southeastern coast, along the Mississippi River, and in the Tennessee region. But the number of escapees continually grew, and more slaves entered Union lines as the army penetrated Confederate territory. Slaveholders in any proximity to U.S. forces feared that they would lose all their slaves. Here a fugitive slave from Maryland writes to his beloved wife after he reaches the safety of Union lines.

Upton Hill [Va.] January ᵗʰᵉ 12 1862

My Dear Wife it is with grate joy I take this time to let you know Whare I am i am now in Safety in the 14th Regiment of Brooklyn this Day i can Adress you thank god as a free man I had a little truble in giting away But as the lord led the Children of Isrel to the land of Canon So he led me to a land Whare fredom Will rain in spite Of earth and hell Dear you must make your Self content i am free from al the Slavers Lash and as you have chose the Wise plan Of Serving the lord i hope you Will pray Much and i Will try by the help of god To Serv him With all my hart I am With a very nice man and have All that hart Can Wish But My Dear I Cant express my grate desire that i Have to See you i trust the time Will Come When We Shal meet again And if We dont met on earth We Will Meet in heven Whare Jesas ranes Dear Elizabeth tell Mrs Own[ees] That i trust that She Will Continue Her kindness to you and that god Will Bless her on earth and Save her In grate eternity My Acomplements To Mrs Owens and her Children may They Prosper through life I never Shall forgit her kindness to me Dear Wife i must Close rest yourself Contented i am free i Want you to rite To me Soon as you Can Without Delay Direct your letter to the 14ᵗʰ Reigment New york State malitia Uptons Hill Virginea In Care of Mʳ Cranford Comary Write my Dear Soon As you C Your Affectionate Husban Kiss Daniel For me

John Boston

Give my love to Father and Mother

Source: An enclosure in Maj. Genl. Geo. B. McClellan to Hon. Edwin Stanton, 21 Jan. 1862, A-587 1862, Letters Received, series 12, Adjutant General's Office, Record Group 94, National Archives. The envelope is addressed, in a different handwriting, to "Mrs. Elizabeth Boston Care Mrs. Prescia Owen Owensville Post Office Maryland."
Published in Berlin et al., *Free at Last*, 29–30.

Northern Black Leaders Urge a Wider Agenda for the War

In the North black Americans faced cradle-to-grave discrimination and suffered from restricted economic opportunities. Well over 90 percent lived where they could not cast a ballot. But at least it was true that free blacks in the North could have their own churches, obtain some education, organize for progress, or start a newspaper or a business. Some prospered, and a well-educated elite became abolitionists or agitated for greater freedom. These African American leaders in the North quickly saw the war as an opportunity to attack many past wrongs, and their agenda was broad and encompassing. It included a deep concern for the future welfare of those in slavery. Here the editor of an important black New York City newspaper, the Weekly Anglo-African, *looks ahead to the needs and interests of Southern blacks, after slavery may be destroyed.*

November 23, 1861

What Shall Be Done with the Slaves?

When the war is ended, there will be few, if any slaves, for the government to dispose of. There will be four million of free men and women and children, accustomed to toil, who have by their labor during sixty years past supported themselves, and in addition, an extravagant aristocracy. . . . Besides these laborers, lands will be confiscated to the government, and turned into public lands. . . . What course can be clearer, what course more politic, what course will so immediately restore the equilibrium of commerce, what course will be so just, so humane, so thoroughly conducive to the public weal and the national advancement, as that the government *should immediately bestow these lands upon these freed men who know best how to cultivate* them, and will joyfully bring their brawny arms, their willing hearts, and their skilled hands to the glorious labor of cultivating as their OWN, the lands which they have bought and paid for by their sweat and blood.

Source: James M. McPherson, *The Negro's Civil War* (New York: Ballantine Books, 1965, 1982, 1991), 297–98.

Frederick Douglass on Prejudice and Slavery

Frederick Douglass was one of the strongest black voices in the North demanding change and progress. He had been born Frederick Bailey, a slave in Maryland, but he escaped to the North and took the last name Douglass. There he became an abolitionist noted for his powerful and impressive oratory. After publishing his autobiography in 1845, he became quite widely known, and his career continued to impress racist whites who found it hard to believe that a black man could have such impressive abilities. Douglass reached large audiences through his speaking and even more people through the newspaper that he published, Douglass' Monthly. Here, in his newspaper, he tries to reason with whites who were coming to see the value of destroying slavery but feared having free black people as a part of society. Profoundly aware of the depth of white racism, he defends black abilities, condemns the nation's history of unjust treatment of African Americans, and appeals for fairness and an end to persecution.

March 1862

My answer to the question, What shall be done with the four million slaves if emancipated? shall be alike short and simple: Do nothing with them, but leave them just as you have left other men, to do with and for themselves. . . . We ask nothing at the hands of the American people but simple justice, and an equal chance to live; and if we cannot live and flourish on such terms, our case should be referred to the Author of our existence. Injustice, oppression, and Slavery with their manifold concomitants have been tried with us during a period of more than two hundred years. Under the whole heavens you will find no parallel to the wrongs we have endured. . . .

Take any race you please, French, English, Irish, or Scotch, subject them to slavery for ages—regard and treat them everywhere, everyway, as property, as having no rights which other men are required to respect.—Let them be loaded with chains, scarred with the whip, branded with hot irons, sold in the market, kept in ignorance by force of law and common usage, and I venture to say that the same doubt would spring up regarding either of them, which now confronts the negro. The common talk of the streets on this subject shows great ignorance. It assumes that no other race has ever been enslaved or could be held in slavery, and the fact that the black man submits to that condition is often cited as a proof of original and permanent inferiority, and of the fitness of the black man only for that condition. Just this is the argument of the Confederate States . . . But what are the facts? I believe it will not be denied that the Anglo-Saxons are a fine race of men, and have done something for the civilization of mankind, yet who does not know that this now grand and leading race was in bondage and abject slavery for ages upon their own native soil? They were not stolen away from their own country, in small numbers where they could make no resistance to their enslavers, but were enslaved in their own country. . . .

The misfortunes of my own race in this respect are not singular. They have happened to all nations, when under the heel of oppression. Whenever and wherever any particular variety of the human family have been enslaved by another, their enslavers and oppressors, in every such instance, have found their best apology for their own base conduct in the bad character of their victims. The cunning, the deceit, the indolence, and the manifold vices and crimes, which naturally grow out of the condition of slavery, are generally charged as inherent characteristics of the oppressed and enslaved race. The Jews, the Indians, the Saxons, and the ancient Britons have all had a taste of this bitter experience. . . .

But to return. What shall be done with the four million slaves, if emancipated? I answer, deal justly with them; pay them honest wages for honest work; dispense with the biting lash, and pay them the ready cash; awaken a new class of motives in them; remove the old motives of shriveling fear of punishment which benumb and degrade the soul, and supplant them by the higher and better motives of hope, of self-respect, of honor, and of personal responsibility. Reverse the whole current of feeling in regard to them. They have been compelled hitherto to regard the white man as a cruel, selfish, and remorseless tyrant, thirsting for wealth, greedy of gain, and caring nothing of the means by which he obtains it. Now, let him see that the white man has a nobler and better side to his character, and he will love, honor, esteem the white man.

Source: *Douglass' Monthly*, 4 (March 1862), 614–15.

Racism and Mistreatment Plague Many Army Camps

In March 1862 the U.S. Congress ordered that army officers could no longer return fugitive slaves to their owners. Congress had decided that the Union should benefit from escaped slaves' help. That change in government policy could not, however, make every racist officer treat the "contrabands" fairly. There were many abuses of both black men and black women. An equally serious problem was the racist indifference or apathy of many whites in the military service. Thus, despite the government's change of policy, contrabands often suffered what one black newspaper called "positively horrible" treatment. Racism was generally widespread, but it was especially strong in units of the western army. Here a committee of white chaplains and surgeons felt compelled to alert their superior to the many abuses suffered by runaway slaves who were trying to help the Union.

Helena Arkansas Dec 29th 1862

General The undersigned Chaplains and Surgeons of the army of the Eastern District of Arkansas would respectfully call your attention to the Statements & Suggestions following

The Contrabands within our lines are experiencing hardships oppression & neglect the removal of which calls loudly for the intervention of authority. We daily see & deplore the evil and leave it to your wisdom to devise a remedy. In a great degree the contrabands are left entirely to the mercy and rapacity of the unprincipled part of our army . . . with no person clothed with Specific authority to look after & protect them. Among their list of grievances we mention these:

Some who have been paid by individuals for cotton or for labor have been waylaid by soldiers, robbed, and in several instances fired upon, as well as robbed, and in no case that we can now recal have the plunderers been brought to justice–

The wives of some have been molested by soldiers to gratify thier licentious lust, and thier husbands murdered in endeavering to defend them, and yet the guilty parties, though known, were not arrested. Some who have wives and families are required to work on the Fortifications, or to unload Government Stores, and receive only their meals at the Public table, while their families, whatever provision is intended for them, are, as a matter of fact, left in a helpless & starving condition

Many of the contrabands have been employed, & received in numerous instances, from officers & privates, only counterfeit money or nothing at all for their services. One man was employed as a teamster by the Government & he died in the service (the government indebted to him nearly fifty dollars) leaving an orphan child eight years old, & there is no apparent provision made to draw the money, or to care for the orphan child. The negro hospital here has become notorious for filth, neglect, mortality & brutal whipping, so that the contrabands have lost all hope of kind treatment there, & would almost as soon go to their graves as to their hospital. These grievances reported to us by persons in whom we have confidence, & some of which we know to be true, are but a few of the many wrongs of which they complain– For the sake of humanity, for the sake of christianity, for the good name of our army, for the honor of our country, cannot something be done to prevent this oppression & to stop its demoralizing influences upon the Soldiers themselves? Some have suggested that the matter be laid befor the [War] Department at Washington, in the hope that they will clothe an agent with authority, to register all the names of the contrabands, who will have a benevolent regard for their welfare, though whom all details of fatigue & working parties shall be made though whom rations may be drawn & money paid, & who shall be empowered to organize schools, & to make all needfull Regulations for the comfort & improvement of the condition of the contrabands; whose accounts shall be open at all times for inspection, and who shall make stated reports to the Department– All which is respectfully submitted

Samuel Sawyer
committee Pearl P Ingall
J. G. Forman

Source: Samuel Sawyer et al. to Maj. Gen. Curtis, 29 Dec. 1862, enclosed in Chaplain Samuel Sawyer to Major Gen. Curtis, 26 Jan. 1863, #135 1863, Letters Received Relating to Military Discipline & Control, series 22, Headquarters of the Army, Record Group 108, National Archives. From Berlin et al., *Free at Last*, 180–82.

U.S. Military Policy toward the Freedmen Continues to Evolve Following the Emancipation Proclamation

In this letter the general-in-chief of the army, Henry Halleck, endorses new policies to General Ulysses S. Grant, then commanding the Department of the Tennessee. Halleck's words show that both practice and thought in the army were lagging behind the views of many Republicans in Congress. Open hostility to African Americans remained a problem to be overcome. Halleck seemed to prefer, as had Lincoln, to use black soldiers in a mere support role, where they would man forts and hold positions while white men did the actual fighting. The idea that black men could be an efficient fighting force was gaining ground, but many still opposed it. General Grant was one officer who needed little convincing on the use of black soldiers. He fully agreed with Halleck that the war had entered a new phase. The Union was turning from a "soft" policy to a "hard war" policy, in which African Americans could gain the opportunity to prove their courage.

Washington [D.C.], March 31st /63

(Unofficial)

Genl, It is the policy of the government to withdraw from the enemy as much productive labor as possible. So long as the rebels retain and employ their slaves in producing grains, &c, they can employ all the whites in the field. Every slave withdrawn from the enemy, is equivalent to a white man put *hors de combat* [out of combat].

Again, it is the policy of the government to use the negroes of the South so far as practicable as a military force for the defence of forts, depôts, &c. If the experience of Genl Banks near New Orleans should be satisfactory, a much larger force will be organized during the coming summer; & if they can be used to hold points on the Mississippi during the sickly season, it will afford much relief to our armies. They certainly can be used with advantage as laborers, teamsters, cooks, &c.

And it is the opinion of many who have examined the question without passion or prejudice, that they can also be used as a military force. It certainly is good policy to use them to the very best advantage we can. Like almost anything else, they may be made instruments of good or evil. In the hands of the enemy they are used with much effect against us. In our hands we must try to use them with the best possible effect against the rebels.

It has been reported to the Secretary of War that many of the officers of your command not only discourage the negroes from coming under our protection, but, by ill treatment, force them to return to their masters. This is not only bad policy in itself, but it is directly opposed to the policy adopted by the government. Whatever may be the individual opinion of an officer in regard to the wisdom of measures adopted and announced by the government, it is the duty of every one to cheerfully and honestly endeavour to carry out the measures so adopted. Their good or bad policy is a matter of opinion before they are tried; their real character can only be determined by a fair trial. When adopted by the government it is the duty of every officer to give them such a trial, and to do everything in his power to carry the orders of his government into execution.

It is expected that you will use your official and personal influence to remove prejudices on this subject, and to fully and thoroughly carry out the policy now adopted and ordered by the government. That policy is, to withdraw from the use of the enemy all the slaves you can, and to employ those so withdrawn, to the best possible advantage against the enemy.

The character of the war has very much changed within the last year. There is now no possible hope of a reconciliation with the rebels. The union party in the South is virtually destroyed. There can be no peace but that which is enforced by the sword. We must conquer the rebels, or be conquered by them. The north must either destroy the slave-oligarchy, or become slaves themselves;–the manufacturers–mere hewers of wood and drawers of water to southern aristocrats.

This is the phase which the rebellion has now assumed. We must take things as they are. The government, looking at the subject in all its aspects, has adopted a policy, and we must cheerfully and faithfully carry out that policy.

I write you this unofficial letter, simply as a personal friend, and as a matter of friendly advice. From my position here, where I can survey the entire field, perhaps I may be better able to understand the tone of public opinion, and the intentions of the Government, than you can from merely consulting the officers of your own army. Very respectfully Your obt servt

H. W. Halleck

Source: Genl. in Chief. H. W. Halleck to Major Genl. U. S. Grant, 31 Mar. 1863, H. W. Halleck Letters Sent, Generals' Papers & Books, series 159, Record Group 94, National Archives. Published in Berlin et al., *Free at Last*, 101–3.

Black Troops Prove Their Bravery

Seizing control of the Mississippi River was a key objective of the Union military. By controlling the river, the North would be able to separate the Confederacy into two parts and prevent areas west of the Mississippi River from aiding the many battlegrounds to the east. Port Hudson, along with the city of Vicksburg, was one of the main Confederate positions on the Mississippi River that Union forces had to conquer in order to split the Confederacy in two. At the end of May 1863 black units from Louisiana went into battle there. The Louisiana Native Guards made a courageous assault under extremely disadvantageous conditions. Theirs was a hopeless effort against impossible odds. But the courage of the soldiers won praise in some Northern newspapers and the lasting respect of white officers like the author of this letter. They were proving to skeptical whites that black men would fight. Eventually Port Hudson would fall after a long siege.

Baton Rouge [La.] May 29th /63.

General. feeling deeply interested in the cause which you have espoused, I take the liberty to transmit the following, concerning the colored Troops engaged in the recent battles at Port Hudson.

I arrived here the evening of the 26th Inst, was mustered and reported to Maj. Tucker for duty–

. . . My anxiety was to learn all I could concerning the Bravery of the Colored Reg. engaged, for their good conduct and bravery would add to your undertakings and make more popular the movement. Not that I am afraid to meet unpopular doctrins, for I am not. But that we may show our full strength. the cause should be one of general sanction.

I have ever believed, from my idea of those traits of character which I deemed necessary to make a good soldier, together with their history, that in them we should find those characteristics necessary, for an effictive army. And I rejoice to learn, in the late engagements the fact is established beyond a doubt.

The following is (in substance) a statement personally made to me, by 1st Lt. Co. F. 1st R[egiment]. La. Native Guard who was wounded during the engagement.

"We went into action about 6. A.M. and was under fire most of the time until sunset.

The very first thing after forming line of battle we were ordered to charge– My Co. was apparently brave. Yet they are mostly contrabands, and I must say I entertained some fears as to their pluck. But I have now none– The moment the order was given, they entered upon its execution. Valiantly did the heroic decendants of Africa move forward cool as if Marshaled for dress parade, under a most murderous fire from the enemies guns, until we reached the main ditch which surrounds the Fort. finding it impassible we retreated under orders to the woods and deployed as skirmishers– In the charge we lost our Capt. and Colored sergeant, the latter fell wraped in the flag he had so gallantly borne– Alone we held our position until 12. o'clock when we were relieved–

At two o'clock P.M. we were again ordered to the front where we made two separate charges each in the face of a heavy fire from the enemies Battery of seven guns–whose destructive fire would have confuse and almost disorganized the bravest troops. But these men did not swerve, or show cowardice. I have been in several engagements, and I never before beheld such coolness and darring–

Their gallantry entitles them to a special praise. And I already observe, the sneers of others are being tempered into eulogy–"

It is pleasant to learn these things, and it must be indeed gratifying to the General to know that his army will be composed of men of almost unequaled coolness & bravery–

The men of our Reg. are very ready in learning the drills, and the officers have every confidence in their becoming excellent soldiers.

Assureing you that I will always, both as an officer of the U.S. Army and as a man, endeavor to faithfully & fully discharge the duties of my office, I am happy to Subscribe Myself, Very Respectfully, Your Most Obt. Servt,

Elias D. Strunke

Source: Capt. Elias D. Strunke to Brig. Genl. D. Ullman, 29 May 1863, D. Ullmann Papers, Generals' Papers & Books, series 159, Adjutant General's Office, Record Group 94, National Archives. Published in Berlin et al., *Free at Last*, 439–41.

Black Troops Faced Greater Risks If Captured

Not only did African American soldiers endure discrimination and harsh mistreatment in the U.S. army, but they also were at greater risk if captured. Slaveholders

and many white Southerners regarded those who escaped to the Union as traitors. The Confederate Congress ruled that black U.S. soldiers, if captured, would be sold into slavery, and Jefferson Davis indicated that they could be turned over to state authorities, who would punish them as insurrectionists. Thus the fate of a captured black soldier would be enslavement or death. President Lincoln initially took the correct position—that all captured Union soldiers must be treated as prisoners of war. He issued a warning that, in case of mistreatment, there would be retaliation against Confederate prisoners, but he did not follow through on his threat. Thus, black troops fought at greater risk than their white counterparts. Here the mother of a soldier appeals to President Lincoln to protect those fighting for the Union. Her appeal is based both on principles of right but also on the fact that her son had taken part in the brave and bloody assault on Fort Wagner in Charleston, South Carolina.

Buffalo [N.Y.] July 31 1863

Excellent Sir My good friend says I must write to you and she will send it My son went in the 54th regiment. I am a colored woman and my son was strong and able as any to fight for his country and the colored people have as much to fight for as any. My father was a Slave and escaped from Louisiana before I was born morn forty years agone I have but poor edication but I never went to schol, but I know just as well as any what is right between man and man. Now I know it is right that a colored man should go and fight for his country, and so ought to a white man. I know that a colored man ought to run no greater risques than a white, his pay is no greater his obligation to fight is the same. So why should not our enemies be compelled to treat him the same, Made to do it.

My son fought at Fort Wagoner but thank God he was not taken prisoner, as many were I thought of this thing before I let my boy go but then they said M^r. Lincoln will never let them sell our colored soldiers for slaves, if they do he will get them back quck he will rettallyate and stop it. Now Mr Lincoln dont you think you oght to stop this thing and make them do the same by the colored men they have lived in idleness all their lives on stolen labor and made savages of the colored people, but they now are so furious because they are proving themselves to be men, such as have come away and got some edication. It must not be so. You must put the rebels to work in State prisons to making shoes and things, if they sell our colored soldiers, till they let them all go. And give their wounded the same treatment. it would seem cruel, but their no other way, and a just man must do hard things sometimes, that shew him to be a great man. They tell me some do you will take back the

Proclamation, don't do it. When you are dead and in Heaven, in a thousand years that action of yours will make the Angels sing your praises I know it. Ought one man to own another, law for or not, who made the law, surely the poor slave did not. so it is wicked, and a horrible Outrage, there is no sense in it, because a man has lived by robbing all his life and his father before him, should he complain because the stolen things found on him are taken. Robbing the colored people of their labor is but a small part of the robbery their souls are almost taken, they are made bruits of often. You know all about this

Will you see that the colored men fighting now, are fairly treated. You ought to do this, and do it at once, Not let the thing run along meet it quickly and manfully, and stop this, mean cowardly cruelty. We poor oppressed ones, appeal to you, and ask fair play. Yours for Christs sake

Hannah Johnson

Source: Hannah Johnson to Hon. Mr. Lincoln, 31 July 1863, J-17 1863, Letters Received, series 360, Colored Troops Division, Adjutant General's Office, Record Group 94, National Archives. Published in Berlin et al., *Free at Last*, 450–51.

Another Problem with the Army:
Black Southerners Are Forced to Work without Pay

In many ways the U.S. army proved unable and unwilling to provide fair treatment for the contrabands or freed people who were helping it in occupied Confederate territory. The former slaves could aid the army through their labor, and commanders often ordered them to go to work at helpful tasks. But racism and indifference to the blacks' conditions plagued the lives of these workers. Different commanders had different degrees of sympathy for former slaves. Some proved hostile because they were outright racists. Others felt that answering the needs of black people was unimportant. Thus, in addition to mistreatment from racist white soldiers, many former slaves received little pay. Often wages owed the former slaves for work done arrived late or sometimes not at all. Here black men and women in coastal North Carolina petition, in the American tradition, for redress of their grievances.

Beaufort N. Carolina Nov 20th 1863

the undersigned Colored Citizens of the town of Beaufort in behaf of the Colord population of this Commuinty in view of the manner in which their Brotheren on oppressed by the military authurities in this Vicenity Respeckfuley pitision you are at the Head of this military Department for a redress of grievunces

Your [politiness] [*petitioners*] disire to make known to you that they and there brothern to the President of the United States are undiscriminatly

inpressed by the authorities to labor upon the Public woorks without compensation that in Consequence of this System of fource labor they Have no
means of paying Rents and otherwise Providing for ther families

Your pitisioners disire futher to Express ther Entire Willingness to Contribute to the Cause of the union in anyway consistant with there cause as
Freemen and the Rights of their families

Anything that can Be don By You to relieve us from the Burden which
wee are nou Labooring will Be Highly appriciated By Your Pitistior[ers]

And your pititioners Will Ever pray Yours Respeckfully & Soforth

[17 signatures]

Source: Robert Henry et al. to Maj. Genl. B. F. Butler, 20 Nov. 1863, Miscellaneous Letters & Reports
Received, series 5076, Department of VA & NC & 18th Army Corps, U.S. Army Continental Commands, Record Group 393 Pt. 1, National Archives. Published in Berlin et al., Free at Last, 208–9.

The Problem of Equal Pay for Soldiers

*Black soldiers had many causes for grievance in the U.S. army, yet they served
faithfully and well. While risking their lives, they encountered racist hostility,
and all too often they had to do the heavy "fatigue" labor or garrison forts and
positions instead of fighting. Unequal and discriminatory pay was a great cause
of resentment. It was wrong in principle, but it also brought suffering to their
family members. In protesting unequal pay, black troops described the serious ill
effects on their family members, who depended on their wages. This protest, from
a black sergeant to the secretary of war, details the problem. It also shows that
the manly protest of black troops had won some sympathy from white troops who
served nearby.*

Fort Halleck Columbus–Ky. Aprile 27th 1864

I Sir by way of Introduction was made 1st. Sergeant of Co. C which was
then denominated as 2nd Tenn Heavey Artillery now as 3d United States
Heavey Artillery, as I wish to state to you, the facts which can be Relied,
upon as I am fully able to prove if necessary I may say to you this Reg. is
a coloured one of Southern Birth consequently have no Education, not so
with my self I was Freeborn and Educated to some extent which makes me
know we know that we have never had our Just Rights, by the Officers
who command us, the white officers of other Reg. here persuaded me to
Join when there were no Reg. of coloured here to Join so I consented and
being the first to sign my name in this Reg. They promiced to pay us the
same wages as was paid the whites & Rations & clothing the same they

have given us clothing & Rations sufficient for the time but have not paid us our Money according to promice the white privates tell us we Should get the same pay as they do but none of us has yet we never have been paid more than Seven Dollars per Month they now say that is all we are allowd by the Govorment of the United States Many of these people have Families to support and no other means of doing it than what they get in this way. Such of those that are not able Bodied men are employed on Govornment work and are paid Ten Dollars per Month We who belong to this *Reg.* have done more work than they on Fatigue and other wise the very Labour that was appointed for them we have had to toil day and night when necessity demands it, I may say to you at the presant our Regimental officers are nearly played out they have been Turned out and their places have not been furnished with other commanders now *Hon.* Secretary of war I wish to ask you not only for my own Satisfaction but at the Request of my *Reg.* is Seven Dollars per month all we Soldiers are to get or may we Expect in the final settlement to get our full Rights as was promiced us at the first

If we are to Recieve as much as White Soldiers or the Regular thirteen Dollars per Month then we Shall be Satisfied and on the field of Battle we will prove that we were worthy of what we claim for our Rights

With this Statement I may close by Requesting your Answer to this for the many Anxious and disappointed men of this *Reg.* I am Sir your obedient Servant

W^m. J. Brown

PS) Direct yours to me in care of *Co.* C. 3^d U States Heavey *Arty.* Care of *Lieut.* Adams of Co. A. 3^d *U.* States Heavey *Arty.*

Source: W^m. J. Brown to Honourable Secretary of War, 27 Apr. 1864, B-582 1864, Letters Received, series 360, Colored Troops Division, Adjutant General's Office, Record Group 94, National Archives. Published in Berlin et al., *Free at Last*, 467–68.

Ex-Slaves Impress by Their Hunger for Education

On the positive side of relations with the army, the ex-slaves' desire to aid the Union and their hunger for education excited respect among many whites. The desire of slaves to better themselves had an impact on many officers and private soldiers. Some sympathetic commanders tried to support and aid the freed people, and chaplains for black regiments usually were helpful. Here one chaplain described the efforts made by his command to support the eagerness of black troops who had been slaves to begin their education. The behavior of the former slaves and their rapid progress in freedom obviously had made an impression.

Port Hudson La April 8th 1864

General: I have the honor to report that I have visited the schools established and organized by you in the regiments of the 2^d Brigade of your Division, and respectfuly submit the following statement of their condition.

There are, at the present time, four schools in successful operation. The buildings, which also serve as Churches and Lecture rooms, are large and comfortable structures, neatly whitewashed, and fitted with well made seats, desks and blackboards. The attendance of the men has been as regular as was consistent with the performance of their military duties, and they have made rapid progress in learning to read and write.

I am sure that I never witnessed greater eagerness for study; and all, who have examined the writing books and listened to the recitations in the schools, have expressed their astonishment and admiration. A majority of the men seem to regard their books as an indispensable portion of their equipments, and the cartridge box and spelling book are attached to the same belt. There are nearly five hundred men in the four regiments of the Brigade which bears your name, who have learned to read quite well, and also quite a large number who are able to write. A short time ago scarcely one of these men knew a letter of the alphabet. Many of the Sergeants who came into the regiment six months ago, entirely ignorant of the alphabet, are now able to make out their own Rolls. Instruction to a considerable extent has also been given in the Geography of the Country, especially as regards the States, their capitals, rivers, population &c. The accomplishment of so much, under the circumstances, is an additional proof of the intellectual capacity of the race. Their extreme eagerness & ability to improve is established.

Chaplains Chase Camp and Paterson have cheerfuly cooperated in the organizing & conducting of the schools, and especial mention may be made of Messrs Seymour Young and North, who were appointed by you as Instructors. In the death of the last-named officer, the Corps and especially the 9th Regt suffers a serious loss.

This excellent movement for the instruction of our soldiers, inaugerated by yourself and rendered successful by your exertions & by a timely supply of books obtained from the North through your influence, deserves the approbation of every friend of the Freedmen, and your personal efforts in their behalf, will be gratefully remembered by us all in the future. I am, very respectfuly Your obt servt

E. S. Wheeler

Source: Chaplain E. S. Wheeler to Brig. Genl. Ullmann, 8 Apr. 1864, D. Ullmann Papers, Generals' Papers & Books, series 159, Adjutant General's Office, Record Group 94, National Archives. Published in Ira Berlin, Joseph P. Reidy, and Leslie S. Rowland, editors, *The Black Military Experience* (Cambridge, UK, and New York: Cambridge University Press, 1990), 618–19.

Enduring Slavery in the Union's Border States

In the border states still loyal to the Union, black people felt a special frustration. They knew the nation was moving toward emancipation, and many Southern blacks had already gained their freedom. But legally the status of slaves in Maryland, Missouri, Kentucky, and Delaware had not changed. The two letters in this section reveal the special frustration these people experienced, as well as how important it was for them to be able to reunite with their family members. The first letter is from a woman in Maryland whose status as a slave frustrated her desire to unite with her family. Until Maryland abolished slavery, she could not enjoy the basic elements of freedom. (The writer of this letter apparently received no response from the president or the War Department.) The second document shows that African Americans in Missouri were in the same dilemma in 1864 as those in Maryland. The author of this letter, a black Union soldier, writes out of love to his children. His words testify not only to the strong emotions that he felt but also to the determination of soldiers to free their loved ones. In many instances black troops took the initiative and used military force to bring close relatives out of slavery.

Belair [Md.] Aug 25ᵗʰ 1864

Mr president It is my Desire to be free. to go to see my people on the eastern shore. my mistress wont let me you will please let me know if we are free. and what i can do. I write to you for advice. please send me word this week. or as soon as possible and oblidge.

Annie Davis

Source: Annie Davis to Mr. president, 25 Aug. 1864, D-304 1864, Letters Received, series 360, Colored Troops Division, Adjutant General's Office, Record Group 94, National Archives. Published in Berlin et al., *Free at Last*, 349.

[*Benton Barracks Hospital, St. Louis, Mo. September 3, 1864*]

My Children I take my pen in hand to rite you A few lines to let you know that I have not forgot you and that I want to see you as bad as ever now my Dear Children I want you to be contented with whatever may be your lots be assured that I will have you if it cost me my life on the 28th of the mounth. 8 hundred White and 8 hundred blacke solders expects to start up the rivore to Glasgow and above there thats to be jeneraled by a jeneral that will give me both of you when they Come I expect to be with, them and expect to get you both in return. Dont be uneasy my children I expect to have you. If Diggs dont give you up this Government will and I feel confident that I will get you Your Miss Kaitty said that I tried to steal you But I'll let her know that god never intended for man to steal his own flesh and blood. If I had no cofidence in God I could have confidence in her But as it is If I ever had any Confidence in her I have none now and never expect to have And I want her to remember if she meets me with ten thousand soldiers she [will?] meet her enemy I once [*thought*] that I had some respect for them but now my respects is worn out and have no sympathy for Slaveholders. And as for her cristianantty I expect the Devil has Such in hell You tell her from me that She is the frist Christian that I ever hard say that aman could Steal his own child especially out of human bondage

You can tell her that She can hold to you as long as she can I never would expect to ask her again to let you come to me because I know that the devil has got her hot set againsts that that is write now my Dear children I am a going to close my letter to you Give my love to all enquiring friends tell them all that we are well and want to see them very much and Corra and Mary receive the greater part of it you sefves and dont think hard of us not sending you any thing I you father have a plenty for you when I see you Spott & Noah sends their love to both of you Oh! My Dear children how I do want to see you

[*Spotswood Rice*]

Source: [Spotswood Rice] to My Children, [3 Sept. 1864], enclosed in F. W. Diggs to Genl. Rosecrans, 10 Sept. 1864, D-296 1864, Letters Received, series 2593, Department of the MO, U.S. Army Continental Commands, Record Group 393 Pt. 1, National Archives. Published in Berlin et al., *Free at Last*, 480–81.

Efforts to Hold On to Slavery

Even after emancipation became a legal fact, some African Americans had to fight for their freedom. Maryland, for example, ended slavery in October 1864, yet many slaves encountered a tactic in which the white-dominated courts aided former slaveholders. In order to hold on to adult slaves, the former masters sought to gain legal control over young black children. Former owners went before sympathetic judges and apprenticed black children, thus prohibiting parents from leaving with their offspring. Blacks protested and fought against this despicable trick. In the document below, a Maryland woman took her complaint to the U.S. army. Many other parents did the same thing, and as a result Major General Lew Wallace issued a special order to block this practice in Maryland.

Bal^{to} [Md.] Novr 14" /64

Statement of Jane Kamper

Slave of Wm Townsend of Talbot County Md.

I was the slave of Wm Townsend of Talbot county & told Mr. Townsend of my having become free & desired my master to give my children & my bedclothes he told me that I was free but that my Children Should be bound to me [*him*]. he locked my Children up so that I could not find them I afterwards got my children by stealth & brought them to Baltimore. I desire to regain possession of my bed clothes & furniture.

My Master pursued me to the Boat to get possession of my children but I hid them on the boat

her

Jane X Kamper (f[*ree*] n[*egro*])

mark

Source: Statement of Jane Kamper, 14 Nov. 1864, filed with M-1932 1864, Letters Received, series 12, Adjutant General's Office, Record Group 94, National Archives. Published in Berlin et al., *Free at Last*, 373.

The Army's Continuing Failure to Care for Many Black Families

Although U.S. army officers frequently required escaped slaves to enlist if they wanted their families to be cared for in camp, the military's promises of care often proved hollow. The army was unprepared for the large numbers of escaped slaves, and commanders often favored military priorities over moral obligations to the freed people. In many cases there were not enough tents, rations, or other necessities to meet the needs of black women and children. In addition, transfers of commanders sometimes removed those who were determined to help the escaped slaves. Often the military's actions were insensitive, even heartless; sometimes they resulted in enormous suffering. The case below, in Kentucky, received an unusual amount of publicity due to the deaths that occurred, but it was not that unusual.

Camp Nelson Ky November 26, 1864

Personally appered before me E. B W Restieaux Capt. and Asst. Quartermaster Joseph Miller a man of color who being duly sworn upon oath says

I was a slave of George Miller of Lincoln County Ky. I have always resided in Kentucky and am now a Soldier in the service of the United States. I belong to Company I 124 U.S. C[*olored*]. Inft now Stationed at Camp Nelson Ky. When I came to Camp for the purpose of enlisting about the middle of October 1864 my wife and children came with me because my master said that if I enlisted he would not maintain them and I knew they would be abused by him when I left. I had then four children ages respectively ten nine seven and four years. On my presenting myself as a recruit I was told by the Lieut. in command to take my family into a tent within the limits of the Camp. My wife and family occupied this tent by the express permission of the aforementioned Officer and never received any notice to leave until Tuesday November 22" when a mounted guard gave my wife notice that she and her children must leave Camp before early morning. This was about six O'clock at night. My little boy about seven years of age had been very sick and was slowly recovering My wife had no place to go and so remained until morning. About eight Oclock Wednesday morning November 23" a mounted guard came to my tent and ordered my wife and children out of Camp The morning was bitter cold. It was freezing hard. I was certain that it would kill my sick child to take him out in the cold. I told the man in charge of the guard that it would be the death of my boy I told him that my wife and children had no place to go and I told him that I was a soldier of the United States. He told me that it did not make any difference. he had orders to take all out of Camp. He told my wife and family that if they did not get up into the wagon which he had he would shoot the last one of them. On being thus threatened my wife and children went into the wagon My wife carried her sick child in her arms. When they left the tent the wind was blowing hard and cold and having had to leave much of our clothing when we left our master, my wife with her little one was poorly clad. I followed them as far as the lines. I had no Knowledge where they were taking them. At night I went in search of my family. I found them at Nicholasville about six miles from Camp. They were in an old meeting house belonging to the colored people. The building was very cold having only one fire. My wife and children could not get near the fire, because of the number of colored people huddled together by the soldiers. I found my wife and children shivering with cold and famished with hunger They had not recieved a morsel of food during the whole day. My boy was dead. He died directly after getting down from the wagon. I Know he was Killed by exposure to the inclement weather I had to return to camp that night so I left my family in the meeting house and walked back. I had walked there. I travelled in all twelve miles Next morning I walked to Nicholasville. I dug a grave myself and buried my own child. I left my family in the Meeting house—where they still remain And further this deponent saith not

his

(Signed) Joseph Miller

mark

Source: Affidavit of Joseph Miller, 26 Nov. 1864, filed with H-8 1865, Registered Letters Received, series 3379, Tennessee Assistant Commissioner, Bureau of Refugees, Freedmen, & Abandoned Lands, Record Group 105, National Archives. Published in *Berlin et al., Free at Last*, 493–95.

Southern Blacks Petition for Rights in Freedom

Throughout the South, African Americans mobilized to gain their rights as the war came to an end. Early in 1865 a Union Convention of loyal whites was drawing up a new constitution for Tennessee. Black Tennesseans were not allowed to participate, but they made their needs and hopes known in the following document. It presented an impressive variety of arguments and showed that the petitioners had a thorough understanding of democratic governmental processes. Later in 1865, when President Andrew Johnson called other all-white governments into being, African Americans in other former Confederate states would have to make their voices heard, as well.

[*Nashville, Tenn. January 9, 1865*]

To the Union Convention of Tennessee Assembled in the Capitol at Nashville, January 9th, 1865:

We the undersigned petitioners, American citizens of African descent, natives and residents of Tennessee, and devoted friends of the great National cause, do most respectfully ask a patient hearing of your honorable body in regard to matters deeply affecting the future condition of our unfortunate and long suffering race. . . .

After two hundred years of bondage and suffering a returning sense of justice has awakened the great body of the American people to make amends for the unprovoked wrongs committed against us for over two hundred years.

Your petitioners would ask you to complete the work begun by the nation at large, and abolish the last vestige of slavery by the express words of your organic law.

Many masters in Tennessee whose slaves have left them, will certainly make every effort to bring them back to bondage after the reorganization of the State government, unless slavery be expressly abolished by the Constitution.

We hold that freedom is the natural right of all men, . . . We claim freedom, as our natural right, and ask that in harmony and co-operation with the nation at large, you should cut up by the roots the system of slavery, which is not only a wrong to us, but the source of all the evil which at present afflicts the State.

In the contest between the nation and slavery, our unfortunate people have sided, by instinct, with the former. . . . We will work, pray, live, and, if need be, die for the Union, as cheerfully as ever a white patriot died for his country. . . . We are proud to point your honorable body to the fact, that so far as our knowledge extends, not a negro traitor has made his appearance since the begining of this wicked rebellion. . . . We know the burdens of citizenship, and are ready to bear them. We know the duties of the good citizen, and are ready to perform them cheerfully, and would ask to be put in a position in which we can discharge them more effectually. We do not ask for the privilege of citizenship, wishing to shun the obligations imposed by it.

Near 200,000 of our brethren are to-day performing military duty in the ranks of the Union army. Thousands of them have already died in battle, or perished by a cruel martyrdom for the sake of the Union, and we are ready and willing to sacrifice more. But what higher order of citizen is there than the soldier? or who has a greater trust confided to his hands? If we are called on to do military duty against the rebel armies in the field, why should we be denied the privilege of voting against rebel citizens at the ballot-box? The latter is as necessary to save the Government as the former.

The colored man will vote by instinct with the Union party, just as uniformly as he fights with the Union army. . . .

This Government is based on the teachings of the Bible, which prescribes the same rules of action for all members of the human family, whether their complexion be white, yellow, red or black. God no where in his revealed word, makes an invidious and degrading distinction against his children, because of their color. And happy is that nation which makes the Bible its rule of action, and obeys principle, not prejudice. . . .

The possibility that the negro suffrage proposition may shock popular prejudice at first sight, is not a conclusive argument against its wisdom and policy. No proposition ever met with more furious or general opposition than the one to enlist colored soldiers in the United States army. The opponents of the measure exclaimed on all hands that the negro was a coward; that he would not fight; that one white man, with a whip in his hand could put to flight a regiment of them; that the experiment would end in the utter rout and ruin of the Federal army. Yet the colored man has fought so well, on almost every occasion, that the rebel government is prevented, only by its fears and distrust of being able to force him to fight for slavery as well as he fights against it, from putting half a million of negroes into its ranks.

The Government has asked the colored man to fight for its preservation and gladly has he done it. It can afford to trust him with a vote as safely as it trusted him with a bayonet.

How boundless would be the love of the colored citizen, how intense and passionate his zeal and devotion to the government, how enthusiastic and how lasting would be his gratitude, if his white brethren were to take him by the hand and say, "You have been ever loyal to our government; henceforward be voters." Again, the granting of this privilege would stimulate the colored man to greater exertion to make himself an intelligent, respected, useful citizen. . . .

One other matter we would urge on your honorable body. At present we can have only partial protection from the courts. The testimony of twenty of the most intelligent, honorable, colored loyalists cannot convict a white traitor of a treasonable action. A white rebel might sell powder and lead to a rebel soldier in the presence of twenty colored soldiers, and yet their evidence would be worthless so far as the courts are concerned, and the rebel would escape. A colored man may have served for years faithfully in the army, and yet his testimony in court would be rejected, while that of a white man who had served in the rebel army would be received.

If this order of things continue, our people are destined to a malignant persecution at the hands of rebels and their former rebellious masters, whose hatred they may have incurred. . . .

In conclusion, we would point to the fact that the States where the largest measure of justice and civil rights has been granted to the colored man, both as to suffrage and his oath in court, are among the most rich, intelligent, enlightened and prosperous. Massachusetts, illustrious for her statesmen and her commercial and manufacturing enterprises and thrift, whose noble liberality has relieved so many loyal refugees and other sufferers of Tennessee, allows her colored citizens to vote, and is ever jealous of their rights. She has never had reason to repent the day when she gave them the right of voting. . . .

Praying that the great God, who is the common Father of us all, by whose help the land must be delivered from present evil, and before whom we must all stand at last to be judged by the rule of eternal justice, and not by passion and prejudice, may enlighten your minds and enable you to act with wisdom, justice, and magnanimity, we remain your faithful friends in all the perils and dangers which threaten our beloved country.

[59 *signatures*]

And many other colored citizens of Nashville

Source: Unidentified newspaper clipping of Andrew Tait et al. to the Union Convention of Tennessee, 9 Jan. 1865, enclosed in Col. R. D. Mussey to Capt. C. P. Brown, 23 Jan. 1865, Letters Received, series 925, Department of the Cumberland, U.S. Army Continental Commands, Record Group 393 Pt. 1, National Archives. Published in Berlin et al., *Free at Last*, 497–505.

Black Leaders in Savannah, Georgia, meet with General Sherman and Secretary of War Stanton

After General William T. Sherman's successful march to the sea through Georgia, he rested his army for several weeks in Savannah. There Secretary of War Edwin Stanton met with him and also with twenty local black leaders. These men, all ministers or lay leaders of black churches and congregations, seized the opportunity to discuss the war and the future of the race. Since Sherman's racist attitudes were well known, one purpose of the meeting was to consider Sherman's relationship with the nearly twenty thousand slaves who had followed his army to the coast and freedom. Blacks made the advocacy of their interests another purpose in the meeting. Their words revealed that they had a keen awareness of the war's history and of political and social realities. Very importantly, the meeting also resulted in Sherman's Special Field Order Number 15.

[New York, N.Y. February 13, 1865]

. . . .

MINUTES OF AN INTERVIEW BETWEEN THE COLORED MINISTERS AND CHURCH OFFICERS AT SAVANNAH WITH THE SECRETARY OF WAR AND MAJOR-GEN. SHERMAN.

HEADQUARTERS OF MAJ.-GEN. SHERMAN, CITY OF SAVANNAH, GA., Jan., 12, 1865–8 P.M.

On the evening of Thursday, the 12th day of January, 1865, the following persons of African descent met by appointment to hold an interview with Edwin M. Stanton, Secretary of War, and Major-Gen. Sherman, to have a conference upon matters relating to the freedmen of the State of Georgia, to-wit:

. . .

Garrison Frazier being chosen by the persons present to express their common sentiments upon the matters of inquiry, makes answers to inquiries as follows:

First: State what your understanding is in regard to the acts of Congress and President Lincoln's [*Emancipation*] proclamation, touching the condition of the colored people in the Rebel States.

Answer–So far as I understand President Lincoln's proclamation to the Rebellious States, it is, that if they would lay down their arms and submit to the laws of the United States before the first of January, 1863, all should be well; but if they did not, then all the slaves in the Rebel States should be free henceforth and forever. That is what I understood.

Second–State what you understand by Slavery and the freedom that was to be given by the President's proclamation.

Answer–Slavery is, receiving by *irresistible power* the work of another man, and not by his *consent*. The freedom, as I understand it, promised by the proclamation, is taking us from under the yoke of bondage, and placing us where we could reap the fruit of our own labor, take care of ourselves and assist the Government in maintaining our freedom.

Third: State in what manner you think you can take care of yourselves, and how can you best assist the Government in maintaining your freedom.

Answer: The way we can best take care of ourselves is to have land, and turn it and till it by our own labor–that is, by the labor of the women and children and old men; and we can soon maintain ourselves and have something to spare. And to assist the Government, the young men should enlist in the service of the Government, and serve in such manner as they may be wanted. (The Rebels told us that they piled them up and made batteries of them, and sold them to Cuba; but we don't believe that.) We want to be placed on land until we are able to buy it and make it our own.

Fourth: State in what manner you would rather live–whether scattered among the whites or in colonies by yourselves.

Answer: I would prefer to live by ourselves, for there is a prejudice against us in the South that will take years to get over; but I do not know that I can answer for my brethren. [Mr. Lynch says he thinks they should not be separated, but live together. All the other persons present, being questioned one by one, answer that they agree with Brother Frazier.]

Fifth: Do you think that there is intelligence enough among the slaves of the South to maintain themselves under the Government of the United States and the equal protection of its laws, and maintain good and peaceable relations among yourselves and with your neighbors?

Answer–I think there is sufficient intelligence among us to do so.

Sixth–State what is the feeling of the black population of the South toward the Government of the United States; what is the understanding in respect to the present war–its causes and object, and their disposition to aid either side. State fully your views.

Answer–I think you will find there are thousands that are willing to make any sacrifice to assist the Government of the United States, while there are also many that are not willing to take up arms. I do not suppose there are a dozen men that are opposed to the Government. I understand, as to the war, that the South is the aggressor. President Lincoln was elected President by a majority of the United States, which guaranteed him the right of holding the office and exercising that right over the whole United States. The South, without knowing what he would do, rebelled. The war was commenced by the Rebels before he came into office. The object of the war was not at first to give the slaves their freedom, but the sole object of the war was at first to bring the rebellious States back into the Union and their loyalty to the laws of the United States. Afterward, knowing the value set on the slaves by the

Rebels, the President thought that his proclamation would stimulate them to lay down their arms, reduce them to obedience, and help to bring back the Rebel States; and their not doing so has now made the freedom of the slaves a part of the war. It is my opinion that there is not a man in this city that could be started to help the Rebels one inch, for that would be suicide. There were two black men left with the Rebels because they had taken an active part for the Rebels, and thought something might befall them if they stayed behind; but there is not another man. If the prayers that have gone up for the Union army could be read out, you would not get through them these two weeks.

. . .

Eighth: If the Rebel leaders were to arm the slaves, what would be its effect?

Answer: I think they would fight as long as they were before the bayonet, and just as soon as they could get away, they would desert, in my opinion.

Ninth: What, in your opinion, is the feeling of the colored people about enlisting and serving as soldiers of the United States? and what kind of military service do they prefer?

Answer: A large number have gone as soldiers to Port Royal [S.C.] to be drilled and put in the service; and I think there are thousands of the young men that would enlist. There is something about them that perhaps is wrong. They have suffered so long from the Rebels that they want to shoulder the musket. Others want to go into the Quartermaster's or Commissary's service.

. . .

In the absence of Gen. Sherman, the following question was asked:

Twelfth: State what is the feeling of the colored people in regard to Gen. Sherman; and how far do they regard his sentiments and actions as friendly to their rights and interests, or otherwise?

Answer: We looked upon Gen. Sherman prior to his arrival as a man in the Providence of God specially set apart to accomplish this work, and we unanimously feel inexpressible gratitude to him, looking upon him as a man that should be honored for the faithful performance of his duty. Some of us called upon him immediately upon his arrival, and it is probable he would not meet the Secretary with more courtesy than he met us. His conduct and deportment toward us characterized him as a friend and a gentleman. We have confidence in Gen. Sherman, and think that what concerns us could not be under better hands. This is our opinion now from the short acquaintance and interest we have had. (Mr. Lynch states that with his limited acquaintance with Gen. Sherman, he is unwilling to express an opinion. All others present declare their agreement with Mr. Frazier about Gen. Sherman.)

Some conversation upon general subjects relating to Gen. Sherman's march then ensued, of which no note was taken.

Source: Clipping from the *New-York Daily Tribune*, [13 Feb. 1865], "Negroes of Savannah," Consolidated Correspondence File, series 225, Central Records, Quartermaster General, Record Group 92, National Archives. From Berlin et al., *Free at Last*, 310–18.

Sherman Creates Hope That Thousands May Gain Land

After his march through Georgia, General Sherman's next planned move was to turn north and invade the Carolinas. He did not want escaped slaves, who had flocked to his ranks, to slow or interfere with his army's operations when he left Savannah. That was probably his main reason for designating vast areas that had been abandoned by Southern slaveholders as available for black settlement. But his decision also had enormous potential significance for the freed slaves. In an agricultural nation, and in a region filled with hostile whites, African Americans knew that gaining land was their best hope for independence. Quickly 40,000 Southern blacks took advantage of Sherman's order.

IN THE FIELD, SAVANNAH, GA., January 16th, 1865.

SPECIAL FIELD ORDERS, No. 15.

I. The islands from Charleston, south, the abandoned rice fields along the rivers for thirty miles back from the sea, and the country bordering the St. Johns river, Florida, are reserved and set apart for the settlement of the negroes now made free by the acts of war and the proclamation of the President of the United States.

II. At Beaufort, Hilton Head, Savannah, Fernandina, St. Augustine and Jacksonville, the blacks may remain in their chosen or accustomed vocations—but on the islands, and in the settlements hereafter to be established, no white person whatever, unless military officers and soldiers detailed for duty, will be permitted to reside; and the sole and exclusive management of affairs will be left to the freed people themselves, subject only to the United States military authority and the acts of Congress. By the laws of war, and orders of the President of the United States, the negro is free and must be dealt with as such. He cannot be subjected to conscription or forced military service, save by the written orders of the highest military authority of the Department, under such regulations as the President or Congress may prescribe. Domestic servants, blacksmiths, carpenters and other mechanics, will be free to select their own work and residence, but the young and able-bodied negroes must be encouraged to enlist as soldiers in the service of the United States, to contribute their share towards maintaining their own freedom, and securing their rights as citizens of the United States.

Negroes so enlisted will be organized into companies, battalions and regiments, under the orders of the United States military authorities, and will be paid, fed and clothed according to law. The bounties paid on enlistment may, with the consent of the recruit, go to assist his family and settlement in procuring agricultural implements, seed, tools, boots, clothing, and other articles necessary for their livelihood.

III. Whenever three respectable negroes, heads of families, shall desire to settle on land, and shall have selected for that purpose an island or a locality clearly defined, within the limits above designated, the Inspector of Settlements and Plantations will himself, or by such subordinate officer as he may appoint, give them a license to settle such island or district, and afford them such assistance as he can to enable them to establish a peaceable agricultural settlement. The three parties named will subdivide the land, under the supervision of the Inspector, among themselves and such others as may choose to settle near them, so that each family shall have a plot of not more than (40) forty acres of tillable ground, and when it borders on some water channel, with not more than 800 feet water front, in the possession of which land the military authorities will afford them protection, until such time as they can protect themselves, or until Congress shall regulate their title. The Quartermaster may, on the requisition of the Inspector of Settlements and Plantations, place at the disposal of the Inspector, one or more of the captured steamers, to ply between the settlements and one or more of the commercial points heretofore named in orders, to afford the settlers the opportunity to supply their necessary wants, and to sell the products of their land and labor.

IV. Whenever a negro has enlisted in the military service of the United States, he may locate his family in any one of the settlements at pleasure, and acquire a homestead, and all other rights and privileges of a settler, as though present in person. In like manner, negroes may settle their families and engage on board the gunboats, or in fishing, or in the navigation of the inland waters, without losing any claim to land or other advantages derived from this system. But no one, unless an actual settler as above defined, or unless absent on Government service, will be entitled to claim any right to land or property in any settlement by virtue of these orders.

V. In order to carry out this system of settlement, a general officer will be detailed as Inspector of Settlements and Plantations, whose duty it shall be to visit the settlements, to regulate their police and general management, and who will furnish personally to each head of a family, subject to the approval of the President of the United States, a possessory title in writing, giving as near as possible the description of boundaries; and who shall adjust all claims or conflicts that may arise under the same, subject to the like approval, treating such titles altogether as possessory. The same general officer will also be charged with the enlistment and organization of the negro recruits, and protecting their interests while absent from their settlements; and will be governed by the rules and regulations prescribed by the War Department for such purposes.

VI. Brigadier General R. SAXTON is hereby appointed Inspector of Settlements and Plantations, and will at once enter on the performance of his duties. No change is intended or desired in the settlement now on Beaufort [*Port Royal*] Island, nor will any rights to property heretofore acquired be affected thereby.

BY ORDER OF MAJOR GENERAL W. T. SHERMAN:

Source: Special Field Orders, No. 15, Headquarters Military Division of the Mississippi, 16 Jan. 1865, Orders & Circulars, series 44, Adjutant General's Office, Record Group 94, National Archives. Published in Ira Berlin, Thavolia Glymph, Steven F. Miller, Joseph P. Reidy, Leslie S. Rowland, and Julie Saville, editors, *The Wartime Genesis of Free Labor: The Lower South* (Cambridge, UK, and New York: Cambridge University Press, 1990), 338–40.

The Destruction of Hopes for Land Redistribution

In both the North and the South, African Americans knew that owning land was the former slaves' best chance to build a successful future. Without land, and living among hostile defeated Confederates, they would remain economically dependent and socially and politically vulnerable. Unfortunately, President Andrew Johnson soon decided that the lands covered by General Sherman's order would be returned to their former owners. Throughout the southeastern coast, African Americans were profoundly disappointed. This heartfelt petition and protest came from blacks in coastal South Carolina.

Edisto Island S.C. Oct 28ᵗʰ 1865.

We the freedmen Of Edisto Island South Carolina have learned From you through Major General O O Howard commissioner of the Freedmans Bureau. with deep sorrow and Painful hearts of the possibility of goverment restoring These lands to the former owners. We are well aware Of the many perplexing and trying questions that burden Your mind. and do therefore pray to god (the preserver Of all. and who has through our Late and beloved President (Lincoln) proclamation and the war made Us A free people) that he may guide you in making Your decisions. and give you that wisdom that Cometh from above to settle these great and Important Questions for the best interests of the country and the Colored race: Here is where secession was born and Nurtured Here is were we have toiled nearly all Our lives as slaves and were treated like dumb Driven cattle, This is our home, we have made These lands what they are. we were the only true and Loyal people that were found in posession of these Lands. we have been always ready to strike for Liberty and humanity yea to fight if needs be To preserve this glorious union. Shall not we who Are freedman and have been always true to this Union have the same rights as are enjoyed by Others? Have we broken any Law of these United States? Have we forfieted our rights of property In Land?– If not then! are not our rights as A free people and good citizens of these United States To be considered before the rights of those who were Found in rebellion against this good and just Goverment (and now being conquered) come (as they Seem) with penitent hearts and beg forgiveness For past offences and also ask if thier lands Cannot be restored to them are these rebellious Spirits to be reinstated in thier *possessions* And we who have been abused and oppressed For many long years not to be allowed the Privilige of purchasing land But be subject To the will of these large Land owners? God fobid, Land monopoly is injurious to the advancement of the course of freedom, and if government Does not make some provision by which we as Freedmen can obtain A Homestead, we have Not bettered our condition.

We have been encouraged by government to take up these lands in small tracts, receiving Certificates of the same– we have thus far Taken Sixteen thousand (16000) acres of Land here on This Island. We are ready to pay for this land When Government calls for it. and now after What has been done will the good and just government take from us all this right and make us Subject to the will of those who have cheated and Oppressed us for many years God Forbid! We the freedmen of this Island and of the State of South Carolina–Do therefore petition to you as the President of these United States, that some provisions be made by which Every colored man can purchase land. and Hold it as his own. We wish to have A home if It be but A few acres. without some provision is Made our future is sad to look upon. yes our Situation is dangerous. we therefore look to you In this trying hour as A true friend of the poor and Neglected race. for protection and Equal Rights. with the privilege of purchasing A Homestead–A Homestead right here in the Heart of South Carolina.

We pray that god will direct your heart in Making such provision for us as freedmen which Will tend to unite these states together stronger Than ever before– May God bless you in the Administration of your duties as the President Of these United States is the humble prayer Of us all.–

- In behalf of the Freedmen
- Henry Bram.

- Committee Ishmael. Moultrie.
- yates. Sampson.

Source: Henry Bram et al. to the President of these United States, 28 Oct. 1865, filed as P-27 1865, Letters Received, series 15, Washington Headquarters, Bureau of Refugees, Freedmen, & Abandoned Lands, Record Group 105, National Archives. Published in Steven Hahn, Steven F. Miller, Susan E. O'Donovan, and John C. Rodrigue, editors, *Land and Labor, 1865* (Chapel Hill: University of North Carolina Press, 2008), 442–44.

~

Selected Readings

The published history of African Americans is incomplete and less well-developed than studies of white America. This is due to the historic effects of racism and to a comparative scarcity of certain kinds of primary source material. For these reasons a number of projects designed to identify and publish significant documents have been very important. Professor C. Peter Ripley led a team of scholars in creating *The Black Abolitionist Papers*, published in five volumes (Chapel Hill: University of North Carolina Press, 1985–92). The fifth volume in this series focuses on the Civil War era. Professor Ira Berlin conceived and launched the Freedmen and Southern Society Project, a massive effort that deserves to be considered the gold standard in modern documentary publishing. Professor Berlin's teams have published more than fifty thousand revealing documents, carefully selected from millions of records in the National Archives. To date six of nine large volumes have come out in print, along with four volumes aimed at general readers and classroom use. Each of the six large volumes of documents begins with a thorough and outstanding historical essay, making these essential to the work of historians. For this book three volumes from the project proved especially useful: Ira Berlin, Barbara J. Fields, Thavolia Glymph, Joseph P. Reidy, and Leslie Rowland, *Freedom: A Documentary History of Emancipation*, Series I, Volume I, *The Destruction of Slavery* (Cambridge, UK: Cambridge University Press, 1985); Ira Berlin, Thavolia Glymph, Steven F. Miller, Joseph P. Reidy, Leslie S. Rowland, and Julie Saville, *Freedom: A Documentary History of Emancipation, 1861–1867*, Series I, Volume III, *The Wartime Genesis of Free Labor:*

The Lower South (Cambridge, UK: Cambridge University Press, 1990); and Ira Berlin, Barbara J. Fields, Steven F. Miller, Joseph P. Reidy, and Leslie S. Rowland, editors, *Free at Last* (New York: New Press, 1992).

Two older documentary collections that are still important and very useful are James M. McPherson, *The Negro's Civil War* (New York: Ballantine Books, 1965, 1982, 1991) and *Minutes of the Proceedings of the National Negro Conventions, 1830–1864*, edited by Howard Holman Bell (New York: Arno Press and *New York Times*, 1969). See also Rayford W. Logan and Michael R. Winston, editors, *Dictionary of American Negro Biography* (New York: W.W. Norton and Co., 1982). *The Proceedings of the First Annual Meeting of the National Equal Rights League* (Philadelphia: E. C. Markley and Son, 1865) is an important source and can be found online. *The Journals of Charlotte Forten Grimké*, edited by Brenda Stevenson (New York: Oxford University Press, 1988), gives insight into the experience of a member of the North's free black elite who went to South Carolina to teach the "contrabands." James Henry Gooding, *On the Altar of Freedom*, edited by Virginia M. Adams (Amherst: University of Massachusetts Press, 1991) presents the writings of a Northern black man who reported on his experiences in the Union army. Also helpful in providing access to primary sources are Ira Berlin, Marc Favreau, and Steven F. Miller, *Remembering Slavery: African Americans Talk about Their Personal Experiences of Slavery and Freedom* (New York: New Press, 1998) and Daina Berry and Leslie Harris, editors, *Slavery and Freedom in Savannah* (Athens: University of Georgia Press, 2014).

Historians who have been part of the Freedmen and Southern Society Project have published important books on a variety of topics connected to African Americans and the Civil War. Among these are Thavolia Glymph, *Out of the House of Bondage: The Transformation of the Plantation Household* (Leiden, UK: Cambridge University Press, 2003); Steven Hahn, *The Political Worlds of Slavery and Freedom* (Cambridge, MA: Harvard University Press, 2009); Joseph Reidy, *From Slavery to Agrarian Capitalism in the Cotton Plantation South: Central Georgia, 1800–1880* (Chapel Hill: University of North Carolina Press, 1992); Barbara J. Fields, *Slavery and Freedom on the Middle Ground: Maryland during the Nineteenth Century* (New Haven, CT: Yale University Press, 1985); Leslie Rowland, *Families and Freedom: A Documentary History of African American Kinship in the Civil War Era* (New York: New Press, 1997); Susan O'Donovan, *Becoming Free in the Cotton South* (Cambridge, MA: Harvard University Press, 2007); and John C. Rodrigue, *Reconstruction in the Cane Fields: From Slavery to Free Labor in Louisiana's Sugar Parishes, 1862–1880* (Baton Rouge: Louisiana State University Press, 2001).

Other valuable and highly recommended scholarly studies are David Williams, *I Freed Myself* (New York: Cambridge University Press, 2014);

Joseph Glatthaar, *Forged in Battle* (New York: Free Press, 1990); Dudley Cornish, *The Sable Arm: Negro Troops in the Union Army: 1861–1865* (New York: Longmans, Green, 1956); Heather Andrea Williams, *Help Me Find My People: The African American Search for Family Lost in Slavery* (Chapel Hill: University of North Carolina Press, 2012); John H. Bracey, *Blacks in the Abolitionist Movement* (Belmont, CA: Wadsworth Publishing Company, 1971); John Stauffer, *The Black Hearts of Men: Radical Abolitionists and the Transformation of Race* (Cambridge, MA: Harvard University Press, 2002); Stephen Kantrowitz, *More Than Freedom: Fighting for Black Citizenship in a White Republic, 1829–1889* (New York: Penguin, 2012); LeeAnn Whites and Alecia P. Long, *Occupied Women: Gender, Military Occupation, and the American Civil War* (Baton Rouge: Louisiana State University Press, 2009); Hugh Davis, *"We Will Be Satisfied with Nothing Less"* (Ithaca, NY: Cornell University Press, 2011); John David Smith, *We Ask Only for Even-Handed Justice* (Amherst: University of Massachusetts Press, 2014); Jaime Amanda Martinez, *Confederate Slave Impressment in the Upper South* (Chapel Hill: University of North Carolina Press, 2013); James H. Brewer, *The Confederate Negro* (Durham, NC: Duke University Press, 1969); John David Smith, editor, *Black Soldiers in Blue* (Chapel Hill: University of North Carolina Press, 2002); Bob Luke and John David Smith, *Soldiering for Freedom* (Baltimore, MD: Johns Hopkins University Press, 2014); Jim Downs, *Sick from Freedom* (New York: Oxford University Press, 2012); Christopher Span, *From Cotton Field to Schoolhouse* (Chapel Hill: University of North Carolina Press, 2009); and three works by the author of this volume, Paul D. Escott, *Slavery Remembered* (Chapel Hill: University of North Carolina Press, 1978); *"What Shall We Do with the Negro?": Lincoln, White Racism, and Civil War America* (Charlottesville: University of Virginia Press, 2009); and *Lincoln's Dilemma: Blair, Sumner, and the Republican Struggle over Racism and Equality in the Civil War Era* (Charlottesville: University of Virginia Press, 2014).

More studies of African American leaders are needed, but students can benefit from a growing number of titles. These include David W. Blight, *Frederick Douglass' Civil War: Keeping Faith in Jubilee* (Baton Rouge: Louisiana State University Press, 1989) and *Frederick Douglass and Abraham Lincoln: A Relationship in Language, Politics, and Memory* (Milwaukee, WI: Marquette University Press, 2001); Waldo Martin, *The Mind of Frederick Douglass* (Chapel Hill: University of North Carolina Press, 1984); Joel Schor, *Henry Highland Garnet: A Voice of Black Radicalism in the Nineteenth Century* (Westport, CT: Greenwood Press, 1977); David Cecelski, *The Fire of Freedom: Abraham Galloway and the Slaves' Civil War* (Chapel Hill: University of North Carolina Press, 2012); William F. Cheek, *John Mercer Langston and the Fight for Black Freedom, 1829–1865* (Urbana: University of Illinois Press, 1989);

John Stauffer, editor, *The Works of James McCune Smith: Black Intellectual and Abolitionist* (New York: Oxford University Press, 2006); Margaret Hope Bacon, *But One Race: The Life of Robert Purvis* (Albany: State University of New York, 2007); Victor Ullman, *Martin R. Delany: The Beginnings of Black Nationalism* (Boston: Beacon Press, 1971); Tunde Adeleke, *Without Regard to Race: The Other Martin Robison Delany* (Jackson: University Press of Mississippi, 2003); and Okon Uya, *From Slavery to Public Service: Robert Smalls, 1839–1915* (New York: Oxford University Press, 1971). All these authors are helping to give African American history the attention and significance it deserves.

Index

hiring out of, 39–40; literacy among, 9; medical care for, 41; news gathering by, 45–46; as nurses for Confederacy, 41; perceived as lazy, 27; plantation mistresses disregarded by, 42; resistance of, 7–8, 41–42, 46–47, 49–51; runaway slaves freeing of, 44–45; skilled work done by, 40–41; slaveholders appeased by, 49; slaveholders attitudes towards, 6–7; slaveholders bargaining with, 46–47; slaveholders conflicts with, 41–42; slaveholders movement of, 45; slavery hated by, 5–6; as spies for Union, 19, 48, 51; treatment of, 7; unhappiness among, 36; Union army assisted by, 47–48, 50–51; Union army relationship with, 47–49

Smith, James McCune: on emancipation, 24; voting rights fought for by, 81

social equality, 83–84

South: Civil War purpose for, 14; cotton economy in, 3–4; free blacks in, 8–9; Northern blacks volunteering in, 86–89; racism after Civil War in, 113–14, 116–17; secession in, 13–14; slavery after Civil War in, 113–14; slavery justified in, 5

Special Field Order Number 15: on African Americans in Union army, 150–52; recipients of, 108; Sherman issuing, 100, 147, 150–52; text of, 150–52

spies, 19, 48, 51

Stanton, Edwin: on contrabands, 23; equal pay for African American soldiers supported by, 68

Supreme Court, United States, 119

territories, slavery in, 12–13

testimony, right to: African American fight for, 81–82, 146; in California, 81; Douglas on, 124; in North, 82

Thirteenth Amendment to the United States Constitution: Congressional approval of, 105; Lincoln proposal of, 98

Thomas, Lorenzo: on medical care of African American soldiers, 71; recruitment of African American soldiers, 56–57; on role of African American soldiers, 59

torture, 44

Union: freedmen neglected by, 74–76; Northern blacks support of, 16; slaves as spies for, 19, 48, 51

Union army: antiblack riots stopped by, 67; contrabands and reaction to, 21; contrabands as labor force for, 16–17, 20–22, 27, 51, 58, 125, 131–32, 136–37; drafts for, 55; impressment of contrabands by, 137; pillaging by, 48–49; plantations seized by, 71–72; racism in, 48, 54, 58–60, 71–72, 132; Richmond captured by, 108; runaway slaves returned by, 20–21, 27; slaves assisting, 47–48, 50–51; slaves relationship with, 47–49

Union army, African Americans in, 62; abolitionists recruitment for, 55; African American support for, 23–24, 55–56; Banks on, 63; at Battle of Milliken's Bend, 63–65; border state recruitment of, 57; bravery of, 70, 133–34; casualties among, 70–71; citizenship of, 53, 145; Confederate treatment of, 60–61, 71, 134–36; Democratic Party opposition to, 67–68; Douglass support for, 24, 54–55; education among, 138–39; Emancipation Proclamation on

~

About the Author

Paul D. Escott is the Reynolds Professor of History at Wake Forest University. Born in St. Louis, he earned his BA degree, *cum laude*, at Harvard and his MA and PhD degrees at Duke University. A member of Phi Beta Kappa, he has benefited from research fellowships from the Whitney Young, Jr., Foundation and the Rockefeller Foundation, in addition to research grants from the universities where he taught.

His writing has focused on slavery, the Confederacy, and Abraham Lincoln, and he is the author of nine books and co-author or editor of nine other studies. Among his most recent books are *The Confederacy: The Slaveholders' Failed Venture* and *Lincoln's Dilemma: Blair, Sumner, and the Republican Struggle over Racism and Equality in the Civil War Era*.